ISBN 978-1-330-13349-1
PIBN 10033982

Forgotten Books is a registered trademark of FB &c Ltd.
Copyright © 2018 FB &c Ltd.
FB &c Ltd, Dalton House, 60 Windsor Avenue, London, SW19 2RR.
Company number 08720141. Registered in England and Wales.

For support please visit www.forgottenbooks.com

English
Français
Deutsche
Italiano
Español
Português

www.forgottenbooks.com

Mythology Photography **Fiction**
Fishing Christianity **Art** Cooking
Essays Buddhism Freemasonry
Medicine **Biology** Music **Ancient**
Egypt Evolution Carpentry Physics
Dance Geology **Mathematics** Fitness
Shakespeare **Folklore** Yoga Marketing
Confidence Immortality Biographies
Poetry **Psychology** Witchcraft
Electronics Chemistry History **Law**
Accounting **Philosophy** Anthropology
Alchemy Drama Quantum Mechanics
Atheism Sexual Health **Ancient History**
Entrepreneurship Languages Sport
Paleontology Needlework Islam
Metaphysics Investment Archaeology
Parenting Statistics Criminology
Motivational

CONTENTS

CONTENTS

ILLUSTRATIONS

HELEN

AS SHE APPEARED TO FAUSTUS

FAUST. Was this the face that launched a thousand
    ships,
   And burnt the topless towers of Ilium!
   Sweet Helen, make me immortal with a kiss.

                                  [Kisses her.
   Her lips suck forth my soul! see where it flies;
   Come, Helen, come, give me my soul again.
   Here will I dwell, for heaven is in these lips,
   And all is dross that is not Helena.
   I will be Paris, and for love of thee,
   Instead of Troy shall Wittenberg be sacked;
   And I will combat with weak Menelaus,
   And wear thy colours on my plumèd crest:
   Yea, I will wound Achilles in the heel,
   And then return to Helen for a kiss.
   Oh! thou art fairer than the evening air
   Clad in the beauty of a thousand stars;
   Brighter art thou than flaming Jupiter,
   When he appeared to hapless Semele;
   More lovely than the monarch of the sky
   In wanton Arethusa's azure arms;
   And none but thou shalt be my paramour!

                    CHRISTOPHER MARLOWE.
            The Tragical History of Doctor Faustus.

CLEOPATRA

ENOBARBUS. When she first met Mark Antony, she
      pursed up his heart, upon the river of Cydnus.

AGRIPPA. There she appeared indeed, or my reporter
      devised well for her.

ENOBARBUS. I will tell you.

    The barge she sat in, like a burnish'd throne,
    Buru'd on the water: the poop was beaten gold;
    Purple the sails, and so perfumèd, that
    The winds were love-sick with them; the oars
      were silver;
    Which to the tune of flutes kept stroke, and made
    The water, which they beat, to follow faster,
    As amorous of their strokes. For her own person,
    It beggar'd all description: she did lie
    In her pavilion (cloth of gold of tissue),
    O'er-picturing that Venus, where we see
    The fancy outwork nature: on each side her
    Stood pretty dimpled boys, like smiling Cupids,
    With divers-coloured fans, whose winds did seem
    To glow the delicate cheeks which they did cool,
    And what they undid, did.

AGRIPPA.   O, rare for Antony!

ENOBARBUS. Her gentlewomen, like the Nereides,
    So many mermaids, tended her i' the eyes,
    And made their bends adornings: at the helm

A seeming mermaid steers ; the silken tackle
Swell with the touches of those flower-soft hands,
That yarely frame the office.   From the barge
A strange invisible perfume hits the sense
Of the adjacent wharfs.   The city cast
Her people out upon her; and Antony
Enthron'd i' the market-place, did sit alone,
Whistling to the air; which, but for vacancy,
Had gone to gaze on Cleopatra too,
And made a gap in nature.

AGRIPPA.   Rare Egyptian !

ENOBARBUS. Upon her landing Antony sent to her,
Invited her to supper : she replied,
It should be better he became her guest,
Which she entreated.   Our courteous Antony,
Whom ne'er the word of ' No ' woman heard speak,
Being barb'd ten times o'er, goes to the feast ;
And for his ordinary pays his heart
For what his eyes eat only . . . .

MECÆNAS. Now Antony must leave her utterly.

ENOBARBUS. Never; he will not.
Age cannot wither her, nor custom stale
Her infinite variety.   Other women cloy
The appetites they feed, but she makes hungry,
Where most she satisfied ; for vilest things
Become themselves in her.

WILLIAM SHAKESPEARE.

Antony and Cleopatra.

JEPHTHA'S DAUGHTER

SINCE our Country, our God—oh, my sire!
Demand that thy daughter expire;
Since thy triumph was bought by thy vow—
Strike the bosom that's bared for thee now

And the voice of my mourning is o'er,
And the mountains behold me no more:
If the hand that I love lay me low,
There cannot be pain in the blow!

And of this, O my father! be sure—
That the blood of thy child is as pure
As the blessing I beg ere it flow,
And the last thought that soothes me below.

Though the virgins of Salem lament,
Be the judge and the hero unbent!
I have won the great battle for thee,
And my father and country are free!

When this blood of thy giving hath gush'd,
When the voice that thou lovest is hush'd,
Let my memory still be thy pride,
And forget not I smiled as I died!

BYRON.

CHORUS. But who is this, what thing of sea or land?
    Female of sex it seems,
    That so bedeck'd, ornate, and gay,
    Comes this way, sailing
    Like a stately ship
    Of Tarsus, bound for the isles
    Of Javan or Gadire,
    With all her bravery on, and tackle trim,
    Sails fill'd, and streamers waving,
    Courted by all the winds that hold them play,
    An amber scent of odorous perfume
    Her harbinger, a damsel train behind:
    Some rich Philistian matron she may seem,
    And now at nearer view, no other certain
    Than Dalila thy wife.

SAMSON. My wife! my traitress! let her come not
      near me.

CHORUS. Yet on she moves, now stands and eyes thee, fix'd,
    About to have spoke; but now, with head declined,
    Like a fair flower surcharged with dew, she weeps,
    And words address'd seem into tears dissolved,
    Wetting the borders of her silken veil:
    But now again she makes address to speak.

    A 2

Enter DALILA.

DALILA. With doubtful feet and wavering resolution
    I came, still dreading thy displeasure, Samson;
    Which to have merited, without excuse,
    I cannot but acknowledge; yet, if tears
    May expiate (though the fact more evil drew
    In the perverse event that I foresaw),
    My penance hath not slacken'd, though my pardon
    No way assured.   But conjugal affection,
    Prevailing over fear and timorous doubt,
    Hath led me on, desirous to behold
    Once more thy face, and know of thy estate,
    If aught in my ability may serve
    To lighten what thou suffer'st, and appease
    Thy mind with what amends is in my power,
    Though late, yet in some part to recompense
    My rash but more unfortunate misdeed.
SAMSON. Out, out hyæna! these are thy wonted arts,
    And arts of every woman false like thee,
    To break all faith, all vows, deceive, betray,
    Then, as repentant, to submit, beseech,
    And reconcilement move with feign'd remorse,
    Confess, and promise wonders in her change;
    Not truly penitent, but chief to try
    Her husband, how far urged his patience bears,
    His virtue or weakness which way to assail.
    Then with more cautious and instructed skill
    Again transgresses, and again submits;
    That wisest and best men, full oft beguiled,
    With goodness principled not to reject

The penitent, but ever to forgive,
Are drawn to wear out miserable days,
Entangled with a poisonous bosom snake,
If not by quick destruction soon cut off,
As I by thee, to ages an example.

DALILA. Yet hear me, Samson; not that I endeavour
To lessen or extenuate my offence;
But that, on the other side, if it be weigh'd
By itself, with aggravations not surcharged,
Or else with just allowance counterpoised,
I may, if possible, thy pardon find
The easier towards me, or thy hatred less.
First granting, as I do, it was a weakness
In me, but incident to all our sex,
Curiosity, inquisitive, importune
Of secrets, then with like infirmity
To publish them, both common female faults:
Was it not weakness also to make known
For importunity, that is, for nought,
Wherein consisted all thy strength and safety?
To what I did thou show'dst me first the way.
But I to enemies reveal'd, and should not:
Nor shouldst thou have trusted that to woman's
    frailty:
Ere I to thee, thou to thyself wast cruel.
Let weakness, then, with weakness come to parle,
So near related, or the same of kind,
Thine forgive mine; that men may censure thine
The gentler, if severely thou exact not
More strength from me than in thyself was found.

And what if love, which thou interpret'st hate,
The jealousy of love, powerful to sway
In human hearts, nor less in mine towards thee,
Caused what I did ?   I saw thee mutable
Of fancy, fear'd lest one day thou wouldst leave me
As her at Timna, sought by all means, therefore,
How to endear, and hold thee to me firmest ;
No better way I saw than by importuning
To learn thy secrets, get into my power
The key of strength and safety.   Thou wilt say,
Why, then, reveal'd ?   I was assured by those
Who tempted me, that nothing was design'd
Against thee but safe custody and hold :
That made for me ; I knew that liberty
Would draw thee forth to perilous enterprises,
While I at home sat, full of cares and fears,
Wailing thy absence in my widow'd bed ;
Here I should still enjoy thee, day and night,
Mine and love's prisoner, not the Philistines',
Whole to myself, unhazarded, abroad,
Fearless at home of partners in my love.
These reasons in love's law have pass'd for good,
Though fond and reasonless to some, perhaps :
And love hath oft, well meaning, wrought much
      woe,
Yet always pity or pardon hath obtain'd.
Be not unlike all others, not austere
As thou art strong, inflexible as steel.
If thou in strength all mortals dost exceed,
In uncompassionate anger do not so.

SAMSON. How cunningly the sorceress displays
    Her own transgressions to upbraid me mine!
    That malice, not repentance, brought thee hither,
    By this appears: I gave, thou say'st, the example,
    I led the way; bitter reproach, but true;
    I to myself was false, ere thou to me:
    Such pardon, therefore, as I give my folly,
    Take to thy wicked deed; which when thou see'st
    Impartial, self-severe, inexorable,
    Thou wilt renounce thy seeking, and much rather
    Confess it feign'd.   Weakness is thy excuse,
    And I believe it; weakness to resist
    Philistian gold: if weakness may excuse,
    What murderer, what traitor, parricide,
    Incestuous, sacrilegious, but may plead it?
    All wickedness is weakness: that plea, therefore,
    With God or man, will gain thee no remission.
    But love constrain'd thee; call it furious rage
    To satisfy thy lust: love seeks to have love;
    My love how couldst thou hope, who took'st the way
    To raise in me inexpiable hate,
    Knowing, as needs I must, by thee betray'd?
    In vain thou strivest to cover shame with shame,
    Or by evasions thy crime uncover'st more.
DALILA. Since thou determinest weakness for no plea
    In man or woman, though to thy own condemning,
    Hear what assaults I had, what snares besides,
    What sieges girt me round, ere I consented;
    What might have awed the best resolved of men,
    The constantest, to have yielded without blame.

It was not gold, as to my charge thou lay'st,
That wrought with me : thou know'st the magis-
    trates
And princes of my country came in person,
Solicited, commanded, threaten'd, urged,
Adjured, by all the bonds of civil duty
And of religion ; press'd how just it was,
How honourable, how glorious, to entrap
A common enemy, who had destroy'd
Such numbers of our nation : and the priest
Was not behind, but, ever at my ear,
Preaching how meritorious with the gods
It would be to ensnare an irreligious
Dishonourer of Dagon : what had I
To oppose against such powerful arguments ?
Only my love of thee held long debate,
And combated in silence all these reasons
With hard contest: at length, that grounded maxim,
So rife and celebrated in the mouths
Of wisest men, that to the public good
Private respects must yield, with grave authority
Took full possession of me, and prevail'd ;
Virtue, as I thought, truth, duty, so enjoining.
SAMSON. I thought where all thy circling wiles would end
In feign'd religion, smooth hypocrisy !
But had thy love, still odiously pretended,
Been, as it ought, sincere, it would have taught thee
Far other reasonings, brought forth other deeds.

                  JOHN MILTON.
                  Samson Agonistes.

QUEEN GUINEVERE

A FRAGMENT

LIKE souls that balance joy and pain,
With tears and smiles from heaven again
The maiden Spring upon the plain
Came in a sun-lit fall of rain.
  In crystal vapour everywhere
Blue isles of heaven laugh'd between,
And far, in forest-deeps unseen,
The topmost elm-tree gather'd green
  From draughts of balmy air.

Sometimes the linnet piped his song:
Sometimes the throstle whistled strong:
Sometimes the sparhawk wheel'd along,
Hush'd all the groves from fear of wrong:
  By grassy capes with fuller sound
In curves the yellowing river ran,
And drooping chestnut-buds began
To spread into the perfect fan,
  Above the teeming ground.

Then, in the boyhood of the year,
Sir Launcelot and Queen Guinevere
Rode thro' the coverts of the deer,
With blissful treble ringing clear.

She seem'd a part of joyous Spring:
A gown of grass-green silk she wore,
Buckled with golden clasps before;
A light-green tuft of plumes she bore
 Closed in a golden ring.

Now on some twisted ivy-net,
Now on some tinkling rivulet,
In mosses mixt with violet
Her cream-white mule his pastern set:
 And fleeter now she skimm'd the plains
Than she whose elfin prancer springs
By night to eery warblings,
When all the glimmering moorland rings
 With jingling bridle-reins.

As fast she fled thro' sun and shade,
The happy winds upon her play'd,
Blowing the ringlet from the braid:
She look'd so lovely, as she sway'd
 The rein with dainty finger-tips,
A man had given all other bliss,
And all his worldly worth for this,
To waste his whole heart in one kiss
 Upon her perfect lips.

TENNYSON.

ELOISA AND ABELARD

Page 13

" From lips like these · what precept failed to move ?
For soon they taught me 'twas no sin to love."

ELOISA TO ABELARD.

ELOISA TO ABELARD

(Abelard, though a canon in the Cathedral of Paris, married Eloisa
secretly. After much happiness and unhappiness they parted, she with-
drawing to a convent, he to a monastery. Years later, a letter of Abelard's
to a friend, telling the history of his misfortunes, was sent to Eloisa, and
occasioned the letters on which Pope founded his poem. Abelard died in
1142, and Eloisa in 1163.)

In these deep solitudes and awful cells,
Where heavenly-pensive Contemplation dwells,
And ever-musing Melancholy reigns ;
What means this tumult in a vestal's veins ?
Why rove my thoughts beyond this last retreat ?
Why feels my heart its long-forgotten heat ?
Yet, yet I love !—From Abelard it came,
And Eloisa yet must kiss the name.
    Dear fatal name ! rest ever unreveal'd,
Nor pass these lips, in holy silence seal'd :
Hide it, my heart, within that close disguise,
Where, mix'd with God's, his loved idea lies :
Oh write it not, my hand—the name appears
Already written—wash it out with tears !
In vain lost Eloisa weeps and prays,
Her heart still dictates, and her hand obeys.
    Relentless walls ! whose darksome round contains
Repentant sighs, and voluntary pains :
Ye rugged rocks, which holy knees have worn :
Ye grots and caverns shagg'd with horrid thorn !

B

Shrines, where their vigils pale-eyed virgins keep,
And pitying saints, whose statues learn to weep!
Though cold like you, unmoved and silent grown,
I have not yet forgot myself to stone.
All is not Heaven's while Abelard has part,
Still rebel nature holds out half my heart;
Nor prayers nor fasts its stubborn pulse restrain,
Nor tears for ages taught to flow in vain.

    Soon as thy letters trembling I unclose,
That well-known name awakens all my woes.
O name, for ever sad! for ever dear!
Still breath'd with sighs, still usher'd with a tear.
I tremble, too, whene'er my own I find;
Some dire misfortune follows close behind.
Line after line my gushing eyes o'erflow,
Led through a sad variety of woe:
Now warm in love, now withering in my bloom,
Lost in a convent's solitary gloom!
There stern Religion quench'd the unwilling flame,
There died the best of passions, Love and Fame.

    Yet write, oh! write me all, that I may join
Griefs to thy griefs, and echo sighs to thine.
Nor foes nor fortune take this power away;
And is my Abelard less kind than they?
Tears still are mine, and those I need not spare,
Love but demands what else were shed in prayer;
No happier task these faded eyes pursue;
To read and weep is all they now can do.

    Then share thy pain, allow that sad relief;
Ah, more than share it! give me all thy grief.

Heaven first taught letters for some wretch's aid,
Some banish'd lover, or some captive maid;
They live, they speak, they breathe what love inspires,
Warm from the soul, and faithful to its fires,
The virgin's wish without her fears impart,
Excuse the blush, and pour out all the heart,
Speed the soft intercourse from soul to soul,
And waft a sigh from Indus to the Pole.
　　　Thou know'st how guiltless first I met thy flame,
When Love approach'd me under friendship's name;
My fancy form'd thee of angelic kind,
Some emanation of the all-beauteous Mind.
Those smiling eyes, attempting every ray,
Shone sweetly lambent with celestial day.
Guiltless I gazed.　Heaven listen'd while you sung,
And truths divine came mended from that tongue.
From lips like those what precept fail'd to move?
Too soon they taught me 'twas no sin to love:
Back through the paths of pleasing sense I ran,
Nor wish'd an angel whom I loved a man.
Dim and remote the joys of saints I see;
Nor envy them that heaven I lose for thee.
　　　Canst thou forget that sad, that solemn day,
When victims at yon altar's foot we lay?
Canst thou forget what tears that moment fell,
When, warm in youth, I bade the world farewell?
As with cold lips I kiss'd the sacred veil,
The shrines all trembled, and the lamps grew pale:
Heaven scarce believed the conquest it survey'd,
And saints with wonder heard the vows I made.

Yet then, to those dread altars as I drew,
Not on the cross my eyes were fix'd, but you :
Not grace, nor zeal, love only was my call,
And if I lose thy love, I lose my all.
Come! with thy looks, thy words relieve my woe,
Those still at least are left thee to bestow.
Ah, no! instruct me other joys to prize,
With other beauties charm my partial eyes,
Full in my view set all the bright abode,
And make my soul quit Abelard for God.

Ah, think at least thy flock deserves thy care,
Plants of thy hand, and children of thy prayer ;
From the false world in early youth they fled,
By thee to mountains, wilds, and deserts led.
You raised these hallow'd walls ; the desert smiled,
And Paradise was open'd in the Wild.
No weeping orphan saw his father's stores
Our shrines irradiate, or emblaze the floors ;
No silver saints, by dying misers given,
Here bribed the rage of ill-requited Heaven :
But such plain roofs as piety could raise,
And only vocal with the Maker's praise.
In these lone walls (their days eternal bound),
These moss-grown domes with spiry turrets crown'd,
Where awful arches make a noonday night,
And the dim windows shed a solemn light ;
The eyes diffused a reconciling ray,
And gleams of glory brighten'd all the day.
But now no face divine contentment wears,
'Tis all blank sadness, or continual tears.

See how the force of others' prayers I try
(O pious fraud of amorous charity!),
But why should I on others' prayers depend?
Come thou, my father, brother, husband, friend!
Ah, let thy handmaid, sister, daughter, move,
And all those tender names in one, thy love!
The darksome pines that o'er yon rocks reclined
Wave high, and murmur to the hollow wind,
The wandering streams that shine between the hills,
The grots that echo to the tinkling rills,
The dying gales that pant upon the trees,
The lakes that quiver to the curling breeze;
No more the scenes my meditation aid,
Or lull to rest the visionary maid.
But o'er the twilight groves and dusky caves,
Long-sounding aisles, and intermingled graves,
Black Melancholy sits, and round her throws
A deathlike silence, and a dread repose:
Her gloomy presence saddens all the scene,
Shades every flower, and darkens every green,
Deepens the murmur of the falling floods,
And breathes a browner horror on the woods.
　　Yet here for ever, ever must I stay;
Sad proof how well a lover can obey!
Death, only Death, can break the lasting chain;
And here, even then, shall my cold dust remain;
Here all its frailties, all its flames resign,
And wait till 'tis no sin to mix with thine.
Ah wretch! believed the spouse of God in vain,
Confess'd within the slave of love and man.
　　B 2

Assist me, Heaven! but whence arose that prayer?
Sprung it from piety, or from despair?
Even here, where frozen chastity retires,
Love finds an altar for forbidden fires.
I ought to grieve, but cannot what I ought;
I mourn the lover, not lament the fault;
I view my crime, but kindle at the view,
Repent old pleasures, and solicit new;
Now turu'd to Heaven, I weep my past offence,
Now think of thee, and curse my innocence.
Of all affliction taught a lover yet,
'Tis sure the hardest science to forget!
How shall I lose the sin, yet keep the sense?
And love the offender, yet detest the offence?
How the dear object from the crime remove,
Or how distinguish penitence from love?
Unequal task! a passion to resign,
For hearts so touch'd, so pierc'd, so lost as
    mine.
Ere such a soul regains its peaceful state,
How often must it love, how often hate!
How often hope, despair, resent, regret,
Conceal, disdain—do all things but forget!
But let Heaven seize it, all at once 'tis fired:
Not touch'd, but rapt; not waken'd, but in-
    spired!
Oh come! oh teach me nature to subdue,
Renounce my love, my life, myself—and you.
Fill my fond heart with God alone, for He
Alone can rival, can succeed to thee.

How happy is the blameless vestal's lot!
The world forgetting, by the world forgot:
Eternal sunshine of the spotless mind!
Each prayer accepted, and each wish resign'd;
Labour and rest that equal periods keep;
Obedient slumbers that can wake and weep;
Desires composed, affections ever even;
Tears that delight, and sighs that waft to heaven.
Grace shines around her with serenest beams,
And whispering angels prompt her golden dreams.
For her the unfading rose of Eden blooms,
And wings of seraphs shed divine perfumes;
For her the spouse prepares the bridal-ring,
For her white virgins hymeneals sing,
To sounds of heavenly harps she dies away,
And melts in visions of eternal day.
     Far other dreams my erring soul employ,
Far other raptures, of unholy joy:
When at the close of each sad, sorrowing day,
Fancy restores what vengeance snatch'd away,
Then conscience sleeps, and leaving nature free,
All my loose soul unbounded springs to thee.
I wake:—no more I hear, no more I view,
The phantom flies me, as unkind as you.
I call aloud; it hears not what I say:
I stretch my empty arms; it glides away.
To dream once more I close my willing eyes;
Ye soft illusions, dear deceits, arise;
Alas, no more! methinks we wandering go
Through dreary wastes, and weep each other's woe,

Where, round some mouldering tower, pale ivy creeps
And low-brow'd rocks hang nodding o'er the deeps;
Sudden you mount, you beckon from the skies;
Clouds interpose, waves roar, and winds arise.
I shriek, start up, the same sad prospect find,
And wake to all the griefs I left behind.

    For thee the Fates, severely kind, ordain
A cool suspense from pleasure and from pain;
Thy life a long dead calm of fix'd repose;
No pulse that riots, and no blood that glows.
Still as the sea, ere winds were taught to blow,
Or moving spirit bade the waters flow;
Soft as the slumbers of a saint forgiven,
And mild as opening gleams of promised heaven.

    Come, Abelard! for what hast thou to dread?
The torch of Venus burns not for the dead.
Nature stands check'd; Religion disapproves;
Even thou art cold—yet Eloisa loves.
Ah hopeless, lasting flames; like those that burn
To light the dead, and warm the unfruitful urn.

    What scenes appear where'er I turn my view?
The dear ideas, where I fly, pursue,
I waste the matin lamp in sighs for thee,
Thy image steals between my God and me,
Thy voice I seem in every hymn to hear,
With every bead I drop too soft a tear,
When from the censer clouds of fragrance roll,
And swelling organs lift the rising soul,
One thought of thee puts all the pomp to flight,
Priests, tapers, temples, swim before my sight:

In seas of flame my plunging soul is drown'd,
While altars blaze, and angels tremble round.
　　While prostrate here in humble grief I lie,
Kind, virtuous drops just gathering in my eye,
While, praying, trembling, in the dust I roll,
And dawning grace is opening on my soul:
Come, if thou dar'st, all charming as thou art!
Oppose thyself to Heaven; dispute my heart;
Come, with one glance of those deluding eyes
Blot out each bright idea of the skies;
Take back that grace, those sorrows and those
　　tears;
Take back my fruitless penitence and prayers;
Snatch me, just mounting, from the blest abode;
Assist the fiends, and tear me from my God!
No, fly me, fly me, far as pole from pole;
Rise Alps between us! and whole oceans roll!
Ah, come not, write not, think not once of
　　me,
Nor share one pang of all I felt for thee.
Thy oaths I quit, thy memories resign;
Forget, renounce me, hate whate'er was mine.
Fair eyes, and tempting looks (which yet I view!),
Long-loved, adored ideas, all adieu!
O grace serene! O virtue heavenly fair!
Divine oblivion of low-thoughted Care!
Fresh-blooming Hope, gay daughter of the sky!
And Faith, our early immortality!
Enter, each mild, each amicable guest;
Receive, and wrap me in eternal rest!

See in her cell sad Eloisa spread,
Propp'd on some tomb, a neighbour of the dead.
In each low wind methinks a spirit calls,
And more than echoes talk along the walls.
Here, as I watch'd the dying lamps around,
From yonder shrine I heard a hollow sound.
'Come, sister, come!' it said, or seem'd to say;
'Thy place is here, sad sister, come away;
Once like thyself, I trembled, wept, and pray'd,
Love's victim then, though now a sainted maid;
But all is calm in this eternal sleep;
Here Grief forgets to moan, and Love to weep,
E'en Superstition loses every fear:
For God, not man, absolves our frailties here.'
I come, I come! Prepare your roseate bowers,
Celestial palms, and ever-blooming flowers.
Thither, where sinners may have rest, I go,
Where flames refined in breasts seraphic glow:
Thou, Abelard! the last sad office pay,
And smooth my passage to the realms of day:
See my lips tremble, and my eyeballs roll,
Suck my last breath, and catch my flying soul!
Ah no!—in sacred vestments mayst thou stand,
The hallow'd taper trembling in thy hand,
Present the cross before my lifted eye,
Teach me at once, and learn of me, to die.
Ah then, thy once-loved Eloisa see!
It will be then no crime to gaze on me.
See from my cheek the transient roses fly!
See the last sparkle languish in my eye!

Till every motion, pulse, and breath be o'er;
And even my Abelard be loved no more.
O Death, all-eloquent! you only prove
What dust we dote on, when 'tis man we love.
　　Then, too, when fate shall thy fair frame destroy
(That cause of all my guilt, and all my joy),
In trance ecstatic may thy pangs be drown'd,
Bright clouds descend, and angels watch thee round,
From opening skies may streaming glories shine,
And saints receive thee with a love like mine.
　　May one kind grave unite each hapless name,
And graft my love immortal on thy fame!
Then, ages hence, when all my woes are o'er,
When this rebellious heart shall beat no more;
If ever chance two wandering lovers brings
To Paraclete's white walls and silver springs,
O'er the pale marble shall they join their heads;
And drink the falling tears each other sheds;
Then sadly say, with mutual pity moved,
'Oh may we never love as these have loved!'
From the full choir when loud hosannahs rise,
And swell the pomp of dreadful sacrifice,
Amid that scene if some relenting eye
Glance on the stone where our cold relics lie
Devotion's self shall steal a thought from heaven,
One human tear shall drop, and be forgiven,
And sure if fate some future bard shall join
In sad similitude of griefs to mine,
Condemn'd whole years in absence to deplore,
And image charms he must behold no more;

Such if there be, who loves so long, so well ;
Let him our sad, our tender story tell ;
The well-sung woes will soothe my pensive ghost ;
He best can paint them who can feel them most.

ALEXANDER POPE.

FAIR ROSAMOND

Page 25

"*Most curiously that bower was built* · · · ·
With turnings round about,
That none but with a clue of thread
Could enter in or out."

FAIR ROSAMOND

FAIR ROSAMOND

WHEN as King Henry rulde this land,
 The second of that name,
Besides the queene, he dearly lovde
 A fair and comely dame.

Most peerlesse was her beautye found,
 Her favour, and her face;
A sweeter creature in this worlde
 Could never prince embrace.

Her crispèd locks like threads of golde
 Appeared to each man's sight;
Her sparkling eyes, like Orient pearles,
 Did caste a heavenlye light.

The blood within her crystal cheekes
 Did such a colour drive,
As though the lilye and the rose
 For mastership did strive.

Yea, Rosamonde, fair Rosamonde,
 Her name was callèd so,
To whom our queene, dame Elinor,
 Was known a deadlye foe.

The king, therefore, for her defence
    Against the furious queene,
At Woodstock builded such a bower,
    The like was never seene.

Most curiously that bower was built
    Of stone and timber strong,
An hundred and fifty doors
    Did to this bower belong :

And they so cunningly contrived
    With turnings round about,
That none but with a clue of thread
    Could enter in or out.

And for his love and lady's sake,
    That was so faire and brighte,
The keeping of this bower he gave
    Unto a valiant knighte.

But fortune, that doth often frowne
    Where she before did smile,
The king's delight and lady's joy
    Full soon she did beguile :

For why, the king's ungracious sonne,
    Whom he did high advance,
Against his father raisèd warres
    Within the realme of France.

But yet before our comelye king
    The English land forsooke,
Of Rosamonde his lady faire,
    His farewelle thus he tooke:

'My Rosamonde, my only Rose,
    That pleasest best mine eye;
The fairest flower in all the world
    To feed my fantasye:

'The flower of mine affected heart,
    Whose sweetness doth excelle:
My royal Rose, a thousand times
    I bid thee now farewelle!

'For I must leave my fairest flower,
    My sweetest Rose, a space,
And cross the seas to famous France,
    Proud rebels to abase.

'But yet, my Rose, be sure thou shalt
    My coming shortlye see;
And in my heart, when hence I am,
    I'll beare my Rose with mee.'

When Rosamonde, that ladye brighte,
    Did hear the king saye soe,
The sorrowe of her grievèd heart
    Her outward looks did showe;

And from her clear and crystall eyes
    The tears gusht out apace,
Which like the silver-pearlèd dewe
    Ranne down her comelye face.

Her lippes, erst like the corall redde,
    Did waxe both wan and pale,
And for the sorrowe she conceivde
    Her vital spirits faile ;

And falling down all in a swoone
    Before King Henry's face,
Full oft he in his princelye armes
    Her bodye did embrace ;

And twentye times, with watery eyes,
    He kist her tender cheeke,
Untill he had revivde againe
    Her senses milde and meeke.

'Why grieves my Rose, my sweetest Rose ?'
    The king did often say.
'Because,' quoth she, 'to bloodye warres
    My lord must part awaye.

'But since your Grace on forrayne coastes
    Among your foe unkinde
Must goe to hazard life and limbe,
    Why should I staye behind ?

'Nay, rather let me, like a page,
　　Your sworde and target beare;
That on my breast the blowes may lighte,
　　Which would offend you there.

'Or let me, in your royal tent,
　　Prepare your bed at nighte,
And with sweete baths refresh your Grace
　　At your returne from fighte.

'So I your presence may enjoye
　　No toil I will refuse;
But wanting you, my life is death;
　　Nay, death I'll rather chuse!'

'Content thyself, my dearest love;
　　Thy rest at home shall bee
In England's sweet and pleasant isle;
　　For travel fits not thee.

'Faire ladyes brooke not bloodye warres;
　　Soft peace their sex delightes;
Not rugged campes, but courtlye bowers;
　　Gay feasts, not cruell fightes.

'My Rose shall safely here abide,
　　With musicke passe the daye;
Whilst I, among the piercing pikes,
　　My foes seeke far awaye.

c 2

'My Rose shall shine in pearle and golde,
　　Whilst I 'm in armour dighte;
Gay galliards here, my love, shall dance,
　　Whilst I my foes goe fighte.

'And you, Sir Thomas, whom I trust
　　To bee my love's defence,
Be carefull of my gallant Rose
　　When I am parted hence.'

And therwithall he fetcht a sigh,
　　As though his heart would breake;
And Rosamonde, for very griefe,
　　Not one plaine word could speake.

And at their parting well they might
　　In heart be grievèd sore;
After that day faire Rosamonde
　　The king did see no more.

For when his Grace had passed the seas,
　　And into France was gone,
With envious heart Queene Elinor
　　To Woodstock came anon.

And forth she calles this trustye knighte,
　　In an unhappy houre;
Who with his clue of twinèd thread
　　Came from this famous bower.

And when that they had wounded him,
    The queene this thread did gette,
And went where Lady Rosamonde
    Was like an angell sette.

But when the queene with steadfast eye
    Beheld her beauteous face,
She was amazèd in her minde
    At her exceeding grace.

'Cast off from thee those robes,' she said,
    'That riche and costlye bee;
And drinke thee up this deadlye draught,
    Which I have brought to thee.'

Then presentlye upon her knees
    Sweet Rosamonde did falle;
And pardon of the queene she craved
    For her offences all.

'Take pity on my youthfull yeares,'
    Faire Rosamonde did crye,
'And lett me not with poyson stronge
    Enforcèd bee to dye.

'I will renounce my sinfull life,
    And in some cloyster bide,
Or else bee banisht, if you please,
    To range the world soe wide.

'And for this fault which I have done,
　　Though I was forced theretoe,
Preserve my life, and punish mee
　　As you thinke meet to doe.'

And with these words, her lillie handes
　　She wrunge full often there;
And downe along her lovely face
　　Did trickle many a teare.

But nothing could this furious queene
　　Therewith appeasèd bee;
The cup of deadlye poyson stronge,
　　As she knelt on her knee,

She gave this comlye dame to drinke:
　　Who took it in her hand,
And from her bended knee arose,
　　And on her feet did stand:

And casting up her eyes to heaven,
　　She did for mercye calle;
And drinking up the poyson stronge,
　　Her life she lost withalle.

And when that death through every limbe
　　Had showde its greatest spite,
Her chiefest foes did plaine confesse
　　She was a glorious wighte.

Her body then they did entomb,
   When life was fled away,
At Godstowe, neare to Oxford towne,
   As may be seene this day.

THOMAS DELONE.

DANTE AND BEATRICE

ONCE more in man's frail world! which I had left
  So long that 'twas forgotten; and I feel
  The weight of clay again,—too soon bereft
Of the immortal vision which could heal
  My earthly sorrows, and to God's own skies
  Lift me from that deep gulf without repeal,
Where late my ears rung with the damnèd cries
  Of souls in hopeless bale; and from that place
  Of lesser torment, whence men may arise
Pure from the fire to join the angelic race;
  Midst whom my own bright Beatrice bless'd
  My spirit with her light; and to the base
Of the eternal Triad! first, last, best,
  Mysterious, three, sole, infinite, great God!
  Soul universal! led the mortal guest,
Unblasted by the glory, though he trod
  From star to star to reach the almighty throne.
  O Beatrice! whose sweet limbs the sod
So long hath press'd, and the cold marble stone,
  Thou sole pure seraph of my earliest love,
  Love so ineffable, and so alone,
That nought on earth could more my bosom move,
  And meeting thee in heaven was but to meet
  That without which my soul, like the arkless dove,

Had wander'd still in search of, nor her feet
    Relieved her wing till found : without thy light
    My paradise had been still incomplete.
Since my tenth sun gave summer to my sight
    Thou wert my life, the essence of my thought,
    Loved ere I knew the name of love, and bright
Still in these dim old eyes, now overwrought
    With the world's war, and years, and banishment,
    And tears for thee, by other woes untaught ;
For mine is not a nature to be bent
    By tyrannous faction, and the brawling crowd,
    And though the long, long conflict hath been spent
In vain,—and never more save when the cloud
    Which overhangs the Apennine my mind's eye
    Pierces to fancy Florence, once so proud
Of me, can I return, though but to die,
    Unto my native soil,—they have not yet
    Quench'd the old exile's spirit, stern and high.
But the sun, though not overcast, must set,
    And the night cometh ; I am old in days,
    And deeds, and contemplation, and have met
Destruction face to face in all his ways ;
    The world hath left me, what it found me, pure,
    And if I have not gather'd yet its praise,
I sought it not by any baser lure ;
    Man wrongs, and Time avenges, and my name
    May form a monument not all obscure,
Though such was not my ambition's end or aim,
    To add to the vain-glorious list of those
    Who dabble in the pettiness of fame,

And make men's fickle breath the wind that blows
    Their sail, and deem it glory to be class'd
    With conquerors, and virtue's other foes,
In bloody chronicles of ages past.
    I would have had my Florence great and free;
    O Florence! Florence! unto me thou wast
Like that Jerusalem which the Almighty He
    Wept over, 'but thou wouldst not'; as the bird
    Gathers its young, I would have gather'd thee
Beneath a parent pinion, hadst thou heard
    My voice; but as the adder, deaf and fierce,
    Against the breast that cherish'd thee was stirr'd
Thy venom, and my state thou didst amerce,
    And doom this body forfeit to the fire.
    Alas! how bitter is his country's curse
To him who, *for* that country would expire,
    But did not merit to expire *by* her,
    And loves her, loves her even in her ire!
The day may come when she will cease to err,
    The day may come she would be proud to have
    The dust she dooms to scatter, and transfer
Of him, whom she denied a home, the grave.
    But this shall not be granted; let my dust
    Lie where it falls; nor shall the soil which gave
Me breath, but in her sudden fury thrust
    Me forth to breathe elsewhere, so reassume
    My indignant bones, because her angry gust
Forsooth is over, and repeal'd her doom;
    No,—she denied me what was mine—my roof,
    And shall not have what is not hers—my tomb.

DANTE AND BEATRICE FIRST MEETING

Page 34

' On my vision smote the power
Sublime, that had already pierced me through
Ere from my boyhood I had yet come forth."

DANTE. " Purgatorio." (Longfellow's trans)

Too long her armèd wrath hath kept aloof
    The breast which would have bled for her, the
        heart
    That beat, the mind that was temptation proof,
The man who fought, toil'd, travell'd, and each part
    Of a true citizen fulfill'd, and saw
    For his reward the Guelph's ascendant art
Pass his destruction ever into law.
    These things are not made for forgetfulness,
    Florence shall be forgotten first; too raw
The wound, too deep the wrong, and the distress
    Of such endurance too prolong'd to make
    My pardon greater, her injustice less,
Though late repented; yet—yet for her sake
    I feel some fonder yearnings, and for thine,
    My own Beatrice, I would hardly take
Vengeance upon the land which once was mine,
    And still is hallow'd by thy dust's return,
    Which would protect the murderess like a shrine,
And save ten thousand foes by thy sole urn.

                        BYRON.

D

PETRARCH'S CONTEMPLATIONS OF DEATH

IN THE BOWER OF LAURA

CLEAR, fresh, and dulcet streams,
Which the fair shape who seems
To me sole woman, haunted at noon-tide;
Fair bough, so gently fit
(I sigh to think of it),
Which lent a pillar to her lovely side;
And turf, and flowers bright-eyed,
O'er which her folded gown
Flow'd like an angel's down;
For you, O holy air and hush'd,
Where first my heart at her sweet glances gush'd;
Give ear, give ear, with one consenting,
To my last words, my last, and my lamenting.

If 'tis my fate below,
And heaven will have it so,
That love must close these dying eyes in tears,
May my poor dust be laid
In middle of your shade,
While my soul naked mounts to its own spheres.
The thought would calm my fears,
When taking, out of breath,
The doubtful step of death;

For never could my spirit find
A stiller port after the stormy wind;
Nor in more calm, abstracted bourne,
Slip from my travail'd flesh, and from my bones outworn.

Perhaps, some future hour,
To her accustomed bower
Might come the untamed, and yet the gentle she;
And where she saw me first
Might turn with eyes athirst
And kinder joy to look again for me;
Then, Oh the charity!
Seeing amidst the stones
The earth that held my bones,
A sigh for very love at last
Might ask of heaven to pardon me the past:
And heaven itself could not say nay,
As with her gentle veil she wiped the tears away.

How well I call to mind,
When from these boughs the wind
Shook down upon her bosom flower on flower;
And there she sat, meek-eyed,
In midst of all that pride,
Sprinkled and blushing through an amorous shower.
Some to her hair paid dower,
And seem'd to dress her curls
Queenlike, with gold and pearls;
Some, snowing, on her drapery stopp'd,
Some on the earth, some on the water dropp'd;

While others, fluttering from above,
Seem'd wheeling round in pomp, and saying, 'Here
   reigns Love.'

How often then I said,
Inward, and filled with dread,
'Doubtless this creature came from Paradise!'
For at her look the while,
Her voice, and her sweet smile,
And heavenly air, truth parted from mine eyes;
So that, with long-drawn sighs,
I said, as far from men,
'How came I here, and when!'
I had forgotten; and alas!
Fancied myself in heaven, not where I was;
And from that time till this, I bear
Such love for the green bower, I cannot rest elsewhere.

LEIGH HUNT.

Trans. from Petrarch.

THEN said the Son of Orleans: 'Holy Maid!
I would fain know, if blameless I may seek
Such knowledge, how the heavenly call was heard
First in thy waken'd soul. . . .'
    'A simple tale,' the mission'd Maid replied,
'Yet may it well employ the journeying hour;
And pleasant is the memory of the past.
    'Seest thou, Sir Chief, where yonder forest
        skirts
The Meuse, that in its winding mazes shows
As on the farther bank the distant towers
Of Vaucouleur? there in the hamlet Arc
My father's dwelling stands; a lowly hut,
Yet nought of needful comfort wanted it,
For in Lorraine there lived no kinder lord
Than old Sir Robert, and my father Jaques
In flocks and herds was rich. A toiling man,
Intent on worldly gains, one in whose heart
Affection had no root. I never knew
A parent's love; for harsh my mother was,
And deem'd the cares that infancy demands
Irksome, and ill-repaid. Severe they were,
And would have made me fear them, but my soul
Possess'd the germ of steady fortitude,

D 2

And stubbornly I bore unkind rebuke
And wrathful chastisement.   Yet was the voice
That spake in tones of tenderness most sweet
To my young heart; how have I felt it leap
With transport, when my uncle Claude approach'd
For he would place me on his knee, and tell
The wondrous tales that childhood loves to hear,
Listening with eager eyes and open lips
In most devout attention.   Good old man!
Oh, if I ever pour'd a prayer to Heaven
Unhallowed by the grateful thought of him,
Methinks the righteous winds would scatter it!
He was a parent to me, and his home
Was mine, when, in advancing years, I found
No peace, no comfort, in my father's house.
With him I pass'd the pleasant evening hours,
By day I drove my father's flock afield,
And this was happiness. . . .

    'Amid the village playmates of my youth
Was one whom riper years approved my friend;
A very gentle maid was Madelon.
I loved her as a sister, and long time
Her undivided tenderness possess'd,
Till that a better and a holier tie
Gave her one nearer friend; and then my heart
Partook her happiness, for never lived
A happier pair than Arnaud and his wife.
    'Lorraine was call'd to arms, and with her youth
Went Arnaud to the war.   The morn was fair,

Bright shone the sun, the birds sang cheerily,
And all the fields looked lovely in the spring;
But to Domremi wretched was that day,
For there was lamentation, and the voice
Of anguish, and the deeper agony
That spake not. Never will my heart forget
The feelings that shot through me, when the sound
Of cheerful music burst upon our ears
Sudden, and from the arms that round their necks
Hung close entwined, as in a last embrace,
Friends, brethren, husbands went.

'More frequent now
Sought I the converse of poor Madelon,
For much she needed now the soothing voice
Of friendship. Heavily the summer pass'd,
To her a joyless one, expecting still
Some tidings from the war; and as at eve
She with her mother by the cottage door
Sat in the sunshine, I have seen her eye,
If one appear'd along the distant path,
Shape to the form she loved his lineaments,
Her cheek faint flush'd by hope, that made her heart
Seem as it sunk within her. So the days
And weeks and months pass'd on, and when the leaves
Fell in the autumn, a most painful hope
That reason own'd not, that with expectation
Did never cheer her as she rose at morn,
Still lingered in her heart, and still at night
Made disappointment dreadful. Winter came,
But Arnaud never from the war return'd,

He far away had perish'd; and when late
The tidings of his certain death arriv'd,
Sore with long anguish underneath that blow
She sank. . . .

   'Bitter art thou to him that lives in rest,
O Death! and grievous in the hour of joy
The thought of thy cold dwelling; but thou
    comest
Most welcome to the wretched; a best friend
To him that wanteth one; a comforter.
For in the grave is peace. By the bed-side
Of Madelon I sat: when sure she felt
The hour of her deliverance drawing near,
I saw her eye kindle with heavenly hope,
I had her latest look of earthly love,
I felt her hand's last pressure. Son of Orleans!
I would not wish to live to know that hour
When I could think upon a dear friend dead,
And weep not. . . .
            'Then my soul awoke,
For it had slumber'd long in happiness,
And never feeling misery, never thought
What others suffer. I, as best I might,
Solaced the keen regret of Elinor;
And much my cares avail'd, and much her son's,
On whom, the only comfort of her age,
She centred now her love. A younger birth,
Aged nearly as myself, was Theodore,
An ardent youth, who with the kindest cares

Had sooth'd his sister's sorrows.   We had knelt
By her death-bed together, and no bond
In closer union knits two human hearts
Than fellowship in grief.

      ' It chanc'd as once
Before the fire of Elinor I sat,
The night was comfortless ; the loud blast howl'd ;
And as we drew around the social hearth,
We heard the rain beat hard ; driven by the storm
A warrior mark'd our distant taper's light.
We heapt the fire : the friendly board was spread :
The bowl of hospitality went round.
" The storm beats hard," the stranger cried ; " safe
  hous'd,
Pleasant it is to hear the pelting rain.
I too were well content to dwell in peace,
Resting my head upon the lap of Love,
But that my country calls.   When the winds roar,
Remember sometimes what a soldier suffers,
And think of Conrade."

     ' Theodore replied,
" Success go with thee !   Something I have known
Of war, and of its dreadful ravages ;
My soul was sick at such ferocity :
And I am well content to dwell in peace,
Albeit inglorious, thanking the good God
Who made me to be happy."

     '" Did that God,"
Cried Conrade, " form thy heart for happiness
When Desolation royally careers

Over thy wretched country ?   Did that God
Form thee for peace when Slaughter is abroad,
When her brooks run with blood, and Rape and
      Murder
Stalk thro' her flaming towns ?   Live thou in peace,
Young man ! my heart is human : I do feel
For what my brethren suffer."

   '"But is there not some duty due to those
We love ?" said Theodore ; and as he spake
His warm cheek crimson'd.   "Is it not most right
To cheer the evenings of declining age,
With filial tenderness repaying thus
Parental care ?"

      '"Hard is it," Conrade cried,
"Ay, very hard, to part from those we love ;
And I have suffer'd that severest pang.
I have left an aged mother ; I have left
One, upon whom my heart has centred all
Its dearest, best affections.   Should I live
Till France shall see the blessèd hour of Peace,
I shall return ; my heart will be content.
My highest duties will be well discharg'd,
And I may dare be happy.   There are those
Who deem these thoughts wild fancies of the mind
Strict beyond measure, and were well content,
If I should soften down my rigid nature
Even to inglorious ease, to honour me.
But pure of heart and high of self-esteem

I must be honoured by myself : all else,
The breath of Fame, is as the unsteady wind,
Worthless."

      ' So saying, from his belt he took
The encumbering sword.　I held it, listening to him,
And, wistless what I did, half from the sheath
Drew the well-temper'd blade.　I gazed upon it,
And, shuddering as I felt its edge, exclaim'd,
"It is most horrible with the keen sword
To gore the finely-fibred human frame.
I could not strike a lamb."

      ' He answered me,
"Maiden, thou hast said well.　I could not strike
A lamb.　But when the invader's savage fury
Spares not grey age, and mocks the infant's shriek
As he doth writhe upon his cursèd lance,
And forces to his foul embrace the wife
Even on her murder'd husband's gasping corse !
Almighty God ! I should not be a man
If I did let one weak and pitiful feeling
Make mine arm impotent to cleave him down.
Think well of this, young man !" he cried, and seiz'd
The hand of Theodore ; "think well of this,
As you are human, as you hope to live
In peace, amid the dearest joys of home ;
Think well of this !　You have a tender mother ;
As you do wish that she may die in peace,
As you would even to madness agonize

To hear this maiden call on you in vain
For aid, and see her dragg'd, and hear her scream
In the blood-reeking soldier's lustful arms,
Think that there are such horrors; that even now
Some city flames, and haply as in Rouen,
Some famish'd babe on his dead mother's breast
Yet hangs for food.   Oh, God! I would not lose
These horrible feelings tho' they rend my heart."

'When we had all betaken us to rest,
Sleepless I lay, and in my mind revolv'd
The high-soul'd warrior's speech.   Then Madelon
Rose in remembrance; over her the grave
Had closed; her sorrows were not register'd
In the rolls of Fame: but when the tears run down
The widow's cheek, shall not her cry be heard
In Heaven against the oppressor? will not God
In sunder smite the unmerciful, and break
The sceptre of the wicked?   Thoughts like these
Possess'd my soul, till at the break of day
I slept; nor then reposed my heated brain,
For visions rose, sent as I do believe
From the Most High.   I saw a high-tower'd town
Hemmed in around, with enemies begirt,
Where Famine, on a heap of carcases,
Half envious of the unutterable feast,
Mark'd the gorged raven clog his beak with gore.
I turn'd me then to the besieger's camp,
And there was revelry: the loud lewd laugh
Burst on my ears, and I beheld the chiefs

PETRARCH AND LAURA AT AVIGNON

Page 38

" How often then I said,
Inward, and filled with dread,
' Doubtless this creature came from paradise ! ' "

LEIGH HUNT   Trans. from " Petrarch."

Even at their feast plan the device of death.
My soul grew sick within me : then methought
From a dark lowering cloud, the womb of tempests,
A giant arm burst forth, and dropt a sword
That pierced like lightning thro' the midnight air.
Then was there heard a voice, which in mine ear
Shall echo, at that hour of dreadful joy
When the pale foe shall wither in my rage.'

ROBERT SOUTHEY.

E

QUEEN KATHARINE

On her trial before King Henry VIII, Cardinal Wolsey, and Cardinal Campeius. She goes about the Court and kneels at the feet of the King.

QUEEN KATHARINE. Sir, I desire you to do me right
    and justice,
  And to bestow your pity on me ; for
  I am a most poor woman, and a stranger,
  Born out of your dominions ; having here
  No judge indifferent, nor no more assurance
  Of equal friendship and proceeding. Alas, sir,
  In what have I offended you ? what cause
  Hath my behaviour given to your displeasure,
  That thus you should proceed to put me off,
  And take your good grace from me ? Heaven
    witness,
  I have been to you a true and humble wife,
  At all times to your will conformable :
  Ever in fear to kindle your dislike,
  Yea, subject to your countenance, glad or sorry,
  As I saw it inclined. What was the hour
  I ever contradicted your desire,
  Or made it not mine too ? Which of your friends
  Have I not strove to love, although I knew
  He were mine enemy ? What friend of mine,
  That had to him derived your anger, did I
  Continue in my liking ? nay, gave notice

He was from thence discharged.   Sir, call to mind
That I have been your wife, in this obedience,
Upward of twenty years, and have been blest
With many children by you.   If, in course
And process of this time, you can report,
And prove it too, against mine honour aught,
My bond to wedlock, or my love and duty
Against your sacred person, in God's name
Turn me away; and let the foul'st contempt
Shut door upon me, and so give me up
To the sharpest kind of justice.   Please you, sir,
The king, your father, was reputed for
A prince most prudent, of an excellent
And unmatched wit and judgment: Ferdinand,
My father, King of Spain, was reckoned one
The wisest prince that there had reigned by many
A year before : it is not to be questioned
That they had gathered a wise council to them
Of every realm, that did debate this business,
Who deemed our marriage lawful.   Wherefore I
    humbly
Beseech you, sir, to spare me, till I may
Be by my friends in Spain advised, whose counsel
I will implore.   If not, i' the name of God,
Your pleasure be fulfilled.

WOLSEY.   You have here, lady,—
And of your choice—these reverend fathers ; men
Of singular integrity and learning,
Yea, the elect of the land, who are assembled
To plead your cause.   It shall be therefore bootless,

That longer you desire the Court, as well
For your own quiet, as to rectify
What is unsettled in the King. . . .

QUEEN KATHARINE.   Lord Cardinal,
    To you I speak.

WOLSEY.   Your pleasure, madam ?

QUEEN KATHARINE.   Sir,
    I am about to weep; but thinking that
    We are a Queen, or long have dreamed so, certain
    The daughter of a king, my drops of tears
    I 'll turn to sparks of fire.

WOLSEY.   Be patient yet.

QUEEN KATHARINE. I will, when you are humble;
        nay, before,
    Or God will punish me.   I do believe,
    Induced by potent circumstances, that
    You are mine enemy; and make my challenge
    You shall not be my judge.   For it is you
    Have blown this coal betwixt my lord and me,
    Which God's dew quench.—Therefore, I say
        again,
    I utterly abhor, yea, from my soul
    Refuse, you for my judge, whom, yet once
        more,
    I hold my most malicious foe, and think not
    At all a friend to truth.

WOLSEY.   I do profess
    You speak not like yourself; who ever yet
    Have stood to charity, and displayed the effects
    Of disposition gentle, and of wisdom

O'ertopping woman's power.   Madam, you do me
    wrong:
I have no spleen against you; nor injustice
For you, or any: how far I have proceeded,
Or how far further shall, is warranted
By a Commission from the Consistory,
Yea, the whole Consistory of Rome.   You charge
    me,
That I have blown this coal: I do deny it.
The King is present: if it be known to him
That I gainsay my deed, how may he wound,
And worthily, my falsehood; yea, as much
As you have done my truth.   If he know
That I am free of your report, he knows
I am not of your wrong.   Therefore in him
It lies to cure me; and the cure is, to
Remove these thoughts from you: the which
    before
His highness shall speak in, I do beseech
You, gracious madam, to unthink your speaking,
And to say so no more.
QUEEN KATHARINE.   My lord, my lord,
I am a simple woman, much too weak
To oppose your cunning.   You are meek and
    humble-mouthed;
You sign your place and calling, in full seeming,
With meekness and humility; but your heart
Is crammed with arrogancy, spleen, and pride.
You have, by fortune and his highness' favours,
Gone slightly o'er low steps, and now are mounted

E 2

Where powers are your retainers ; and your words,
Domestics to you, serve your will, as 't please
Yourself pronounce their office.   I must tell you,
You tender more your person's honour than
Your high profession spiritual : that again
I do refuse you for my judge, and here,
Before you all, appeal unto the Pope,
To bring my whole cause 'fore his Holiness,
And to be judged by him. . . .

[*She goes from the Court.*

KING HENRY.   . . . Go thy ways, Kate :
The man i' the world who shall report he has
A better wife, let him in nought be trusted
For speaking false in that.   Thou art, alone,
If thy rare qualities, sweet gentleness,
Thy meekness saint-like, wife-like government,
Obeying in commanding, and thy parts
Sovereign and pious else, could speak thee out,
The Queen of earthly Queens.   She 's noble born ;
And like her true nobility she has
Carried herself towards me.

SHAKESPEARE.
King Henry VIII.

THE QUEEN'S MARIE

MARIE HAMILTON's to the kirk gane,
    Wi' ribbons on her hair;
The king thought mair o' Marie Hamilton
    Than ony that were there.

Marie Hamilton's to the kirk gane,
    Wi' ribbons on her breast;
The king thought mair o' Marie Hamilton
    Than he listened to the priest.

Marie Hamilton's to the kirk gane,
    Wi' gluves upon her hands;
The king thought mair o' Marie Hamilton
    Than the queen and a' her lands.

She hadna been about the king's court
    A month but barely one,
Till she was beloved by a' the king's court,
    And the king the only man.

She hadna been about the king's court
    A month but barely three,
Till frae the king's court Marie Hamilton,
    Marie Hamilton durst na be.

The king is to the Abbey gane,
    To pu' the Abbey tree;
To scale the babe from Marie's heart,
    But the thing it wadna be.

O she had row'd it in her apron,
    And set it on the sea;
'Gae sink ye or swim ye, bonny babe,
    Ye 'se get na mair o' me.'

Word is to the kitchen gane,
    And word is to the ha',
And word is to the noble room
    Among the ladyes a',
That a babe to Marie Hamilton is born,
    And the bonny babe 's mist and awa'.

Scarcely had she lain down again,
    And scarcely fa'n asleep,
When up there started our gude queen,
    Just at her bed-feet;
Saying, 'Marie Hamilton, where 's your babe?
    For I am sure I heard it greet.'

'O no, O no, my noble queen!
    Think no such thing to be;
'Twas but a stitch into my side,
    And sair it troubles me.'

'Get up, get up, Marie Hamilton;
  Get up and follow me;
For I am going to Edinburgh town,
  A rich wedding for to see.'

O slowly, slowly raise she up,
  And slowly put she on;
And slowly rode she out the way,
  Wi' many a weary groan.

The queen was clad in scarlet,
  Her merry maids all in green,
And every town that they cam' to,
  Took Marie for the queen.

'Ride hooly, hooly, gentlemen,
  Ride hooly now wi' me!
For never, I am sure, a wearier bird
  Rade in your companie.'

But little wist Marie Hamilton,
  When she rode on the brown,
That she was ga'en to Edinburgh town,
  And a' to be put down.

'Why weep ye so, ye burgess wives,
  Why look ye so on me?
O, I am going to Edinburgh town,
  A rich wedding for to see.'

When she gaed up the Tolbooth stairs,
    The corks frae her heels did flee ;
And lang or e'er she cam' down again,
    She was condemned to dee.

When she cam' to the Netherbow port,
    She laughed loud laughters three ;
But when she cam' to the gallows-foot,
    The tears blinded her e'e.

' Yestreen the queen had four Maries,
    The night she 'll hae but three ;
There was Marie Seaton, and Marie Beaton,
    And Marie Carmichael, and me.

' O, often have I dressed my queen,
    And put gold upon her hair ;
And now I 've gotten for my reward
    The gallows to be my share.

' Often have I dressed my queen,
    And often made her bed ;
But now I 've gotten for my reward
    The gallows tree to tread.

' I charge ye all, ye mariners,
    When ye sail ower the faem,
Let neither my father nor mother get wit
    But that I 'm coming hame.

'I charge ye all, ye mariners,
    That sail upon the sea,
Let neither my father nor mother get wit
    This dog's death I'm to dee.

'For if my father and mother got wit,
    And my bold brethren three,
O mickle wad be the gude red blude
    This day wad be spilt for me!

'O little did my mother ken,
    The day she cradled me,
The lands I was to travel in,
    Or the death I was to dee!'

                       ANONYMOUS.

'FOLLOW me closely, Varney,' said the Earl of Leicester, who had stood aloof for a moment to mark the reception of Sussex; and, advancing to the entrance, he was about to pass on, when Varney, who was close behind him, dressed out in the utmost bravery of the day, was stopped by the usher, as Tressilian and Blount had been before him. 'How is this, Master Bowyer?' said the Earl of Leicester. 'Know you who I am, and that this is my friend and follower?'

'Your lordship will pardon me,' replied Bowyer, stoutly; 'my orders are precise, and limit me to a strict discharge of my duty.'

'Thou art a partial knave,' said Leicester, the blood mounting to his face, 'to do me this dishonour, when you but now admitted a follower of my Lord of Sussex.'

'My lord,' said Bowyer, 'Master Raleigh is newly admitted a sworn servant of her Grace, and to him my orders did not apply.'

'Thou art a knave—an ungrateful knave,' said Leicester; 'but he that hath done, can undo—thou shalt not prank thee in thy authority long!'

This threat he uttered aloud, with less than his usual policy and discretion, and having done so, he

Page 41

"*I have heard*
Strange voices in the evening wind ; strange forms,
Dimly discovered, thronged the twilight air."

SOUTHEY. "Joan of Arc"

entered the presence-chamber, and made his reverence
to the queen, who, attired with even more than her
usual splendour, and surrounded by those nobles and
statesmen whose courage and wisdom have rendered
her reign immortal, stood ready to receive the homage
of her subjects. She graciously returned obeisance
of the favourite earl, and looked alternately at him
and at Sussex, as if about to speak, when Bowyer, a
man whose spirit could not brook the insult he had
so openly received from Leicester, in the discharge
of his office, advanced with his black rod in his hand,
and knelt down before her.

'Why, how now, Bowyer,' said Elizabeth, 'thy
courtesy seems strangely timed!'

'My liege sovereign,' he said, while every courtier
around trembled at his audacity, 'I come but to ask
whether, in the discharge of my office, I am to obey
your Highness' commands, or those of the Earl of
Leicester, who has publicly menaced me with his
displeasure, and treated me with disparaging terms,
because I denied entry to one of his followers, in
obedience to your Grace's precise orders?'

The spirit of Henry VIII. was instantly aroused in
the bosom of his daughter, and she turned on
Leicester with a severity which appalled him, as
well as all his followers.

'God's death! my lord,' such was her emphatic
phrase, 'what means this? We have thought well
of you, and brought you near to our person; but it
was not that you might hide the sun from our other

F

faithful subjects. Who gave you licence to contradict our orders, or control our officers? I will have in this court, ay, and in this realm, but one mistress, and no master. Look to it that Master Bowyer sustains no harm for his duty to me faithfully discharged; for, as I am a Christian woman and crowned queen, I will hold you dearly answerable.—Go, Bowyer, you have done the part of an honest man and a true subject. We will brook no mayor of the palace here.'

Bowyer kissed the hand which she extended towards him, and withdrew to his post, astonished at the success of his own audacity. A smile of triumph pervaded the faction of Sussex; that of Leicester seemed proportionally dismayed, and the favourite himself, assuming an aspect of the deepest humility, did not even attempt a word in his own exculpation.

He acted wisely; for it was the policy of Elizabeth to humble, not to disgrace him, and it was prudent to suffer her, without opposition or reply, to glory in the exertion of her authority. The dignity of the queen was gratified, and the woman began soon to feel for the mortification which she had imposed on her favourite. Her keen eye also observed the secret looks of congratulation exchanged amongst those who favoured Sussex, and it was no part of her policy to give either party a decisive triumph.

'What I say to my Lord of Leicester,' she said, after a moment's pause, 'I say also to you, my Lord

of Sussex. You also must needs ruffle in the court
of England, at the head of a faction of your own?'

'My followers, gracious princess,' said Sussex, 'have
indeed ruffled in your cause in Ireland, in Scotland,
and against yonder rebellious earls in the north. I
am ignorant that——'

'Do you bandy looks and words with me, my lord?'
said the queen, interrupting him; 'methinks you
might learn of my Lord of Leicester the modesty to
be silent, at least, under our censure. I say, my lord,
that my grandfather and father, in their wisdom,
debarred the nobles of this civilised land from
travelling with such disorderly retinues; and think
you that because I wear a coif, their sceptre has in
my hand been changed into a distaff? I tell you, no
king in Christendom will less brook his court to be
cumbered, his people oppressed, and his kingdom's
peace disturbed by the arrogance of overgrown power,
than she who now speaks with you.—My Lord of
Leicester, and you, my Lord of Sussex, I command
you both to be friends with each other; or by the
crown I wear, you shall find an enemy who will be
too strong for both of you!'

'Madam,' said the Earl of Leicester, 'you who
are yourself the fountain of honour, know best what
is due to mine. I place it at your disposal, and only
say, that the terms on which I have stood with my
Lord of Sussex have not been of my seeking; nor had
he cause to think me his enemy, until he had done
me gross wrong.'

'For me, madam,' said the Earl of Sussex, 'I cannot appeal from your sovereign pleasure; but I were well content my Lord of Leicester should say in what I have, as he terms it, wronged him, since my tongue never spoke the word that I would not willingly justify either on foot or horseback.'

'And for me,' said Leicester, 'always under my gracious sovereign's pleasure, my hand shall be as ready to make good my words as that of any man who ever wrote himself Ratcliffe.'

'My lords,' said the queen, 'these are no terms for this presence; and if you cannot keep your temper we will find means to keep both that and you close enough. Let me see you join hands, my lords, and forget your idle animosities.'

The two rivals looked at each other with reluctant eyes, each unwilling to make the first advance to execute the queen's will.

'Sussex,' said Elizabeth, 'I entreat—Leicester, I command you.'

Yet, so were her words accented, that the entreaty sounded like command, and the command like entreaty. They remained still and stubborn, until she raised her voice to a height which argued at once impatience and absolute command.

'Sir Henry Lee,' she said to an officer in attendance, 'have a guard in present readiness, and man a barge instantly.—My Lords of Sussex and Leicester, I bid you once more to join hands—and, God's death! he that refuses shall taste of our Tower fare ere he see our face again. I will lower your proud hearts ere we part, and that I promise, on the word of a queen!'

'The prison,' said Leicester, 'might be borne, but to lose your Grace's presence, were to lose light and life at once.—Here, Sussex, is my hand.'

'And here,' said Sussex, 'is mine in truth and honesty; but——'

'Nay, under favour, you shall add no more,' said the queen. 'Why, this is as it should be,' she added, looking on them more favourably, 'and when you, the shepherds of the people, unite to protect them, it shall be well with the flock we rule over.'

SIR WALTER SCOTT.
Kenilworth.

UNA AND THE RED CROSS KNIGHT

A GENTLE knight was pricking on the plain,
Yclad in many arms and silver shield,
Wherein old dints of deep wounds did remain,
The cruel marks of many a bloody field ;
Yet arms till that time did he never wield :
His angry steed did chide his foaming bit,
As much disdaining to the curb to yield :
Full jolly knight he seem'd, and fair did sit,
As one for knightly jousts and fierce encounters fit.

And on his breast a bloody cross he bore,
The dear remembrance of his dying Lord,
For whose sweet sake that glorious badge he wore,
And dead, as living, ever Him adored ;
Upon his shield the like was also scored,
For sovereign hope, which in his help he had ;
Right faithful, true he was in deed and word ;
But of his cheer did seem too solemn sad ;
Yet nothing did he dread, but ever was ydrad.

Upon a great adventure he was bound,
That greatest Gloriana to him gave
(That greatest glorious Queen of Fairy land),
To win him worship, and her grace to have,
Which of all earthly things he most did crave.

And ever as he rode, his heart did yearn
To prove his puissance in battle brave
Upon his foe, and his new force to learn;
Upon his foe, a dragon horrible and stern.

A lovely lady rode him fair beside,
Upon a lowly ass more white than snow;
Yet she much whiter; but the same did hide
Under a veil that wimpled was full low;
And over all a black stole she did throw,
As one that inly mourn'd; so was she sad,
And heavy sate upon her palfrey slow;
Seemèd in heart some hidden care she had;
And by her in a line a milk-white lamb she lad.

So pure and innocent, as that same lamb,
She was in life and every virtuous lore,
And by descent from royal lineage came
Of ancient kings and queens, that had of yore
Their sceptres stretch'd from east to western shore,
And all the world in their subjection held;
Till that infernal fiend with foul uproar
Forwasted all their land, and them expell'd;
Whom to avenge, she had this knight from far
    compell'd.

EDMUND SPENSER.

The Faeric Queene.

BOTTOM AND TITANIA

SCENE: *The Wood.*

*Titania asleep. Bottom transformed by Puck's magic and
wearing the head of an ass.*

BOTTOM. I see their knavery. This is to make an ass
of me; to fright me, if they could. But I will
not stir from this place, do what they can. I will
walk up and down here, and I will sing, that they
shall hear I am not afraid.   [*Sings.*

> *The ousel-cock, so black of hue,*
> * With orange-tawny bill;*
> *The throstle with his note so true,*
> * The wren with little quill;—*

TITANIA [*awaking*]. What angel wakes me from my
flowery bed?

BOT.   *The finch, the sparrow, and the lark;*
> * The plain-song cuckoo gray,*
> *Whose note full many a man doth mark,*
> * And dares not answer, nay;—*

for, indeed, who would set his wit to so foolish a
bird? who would give a bird the lie, though he
cry 'cuckoo' never so?

TITA. I pray thee, gentle mortal, sing again:
Mine ear is much enamoured of thy note;

So is mine eye enthrallèd to thy shape;
And thy fair virtue's force, perforce, doth move
me,
On the first view, to say, to swear, I love thee.

Bot. Methinks, mistress, you should have little
reason for that, and yet, to say the truth, reason
and love keep little company together now-a-
days:—the more the pity, that some honest neigh-
bours will not make them friends. Nay, I can
gleek upon occasion.

Tita. Thou art as wise as thou art beautiful.

Bot. Not so, neither; but if I had wit enough to get
out of this wood, I have enough to serve mine
own turn.

Tita. Out of this wood do not desire to go:
Thou shalt remain here, whether thou wilt or no.
I am a spirit of no common rate,—
The summer still doth tend upon my state,—
And I do love thee: therefore, go with me;
I'll give thee fairies to attend on thee;
And they shall fetch thee jewels from the deep,
And sing while thou on pressèd flowers dost sleep;
And I will purge thy mortal grossness so,
That thou shalt like an airy spirit go.—
Pease-blossom! Cobweb! Moth! and Mustard-
seed!

Enter four FAIRIES.

1st Fai. Ready.
2nd Fai.   And I.

3RD FAI.　　　　　　　And I.

4TH FAI.　　　　　　　　　　Where shall we go?

TITA. Be kind and courteous to this gentleman
　　　Hop in his walks, and gambol in his eyes;
　　　Feed him with apricocks, and dewberries,
　　　With purple grapes, green figs, and mulberries.
　　　The honey-bags steal from the humble-bees,
　　　And for night-tapers crop their waxen thighs,
　　　And light them at the fiery glow-worm's eyes,
　　　To have my love to bed, and to arise;
　　　And pluck the wings from painted butterflies,
　　　To fan the moonbeams from his sleeping eyes.
　　　Nod to him, elves, and do him courtesies.

1ST FAI. Hail, mortal!

2ND FAI. Hail!

3RD FAI. Hail!

4TH FAI. Hail!

BOT. I cry your worships mercy, heartily.—I beseech
　　　your worship's name.

COB. Cobweb.

BOT. I shall desire you of more acquaintance, good
　　　Master Cobweb. If I cut my finger, I shall
　　　make bold with you. Your name, honest gentle-
　　　man?

PEAS. Pease-blossom.

BOT. I pray you, commend me to Mistress Squash,
　　　your mother, and to Master Peascod, your father.
　　　Good Master Pease-blossom, I shall desire you of
　　　more acquaintance too.—Your name, I beseech
　　　you, sir?

Mus. Mustard-seed.

Bot. Good Master Mustard-seed, I know your patience
well: the same cowardly, giant-like ox-beef hath
devoured many a gentleman of your house. I
promise you, your kindred hath made my eyes
water ere now. I desire you more acquaintance,
good Master Mustard-seed.

Tita. Come, wait upon him; lead him to my bower.
The moon, methinks, looks with a watery eye;
And when she weeps, weeps every little flower,
Lamenting some enforcèd chastity.
Tie up my lover's tongue, bring him silently.

[*Exeunt.*

Scene. *Another part of the Wood.*

Enter Oberon.

Obe. I wonder, if Titania be awaked;
Then, what it was that next came in her eye,
Which she must dote on in extremity.
Here comes my messenger.

Enter Puck.

How now, mad spirit?
What night-rule now about this haunted grove?

Puck. My mistress with a monster is in love.
Near to her close and consecrated bower,
While she was in her dull and sleeping hour,

A crew of patches, rude mechanicals,
That work for bread upon Athenian stalls,
Were met together to rehearse a play,
Intended for great Theseus' nuptial day.
The shallowest thick-skin of that barren sort,
Who Pyramus presented in their sport,
Forsook his scene, and entered in a brake,
When I did him at this advantage take ;
An ass's nowl I fixèd on his head :
Anon, his Thisbe must be answerèd,
And forth my mimic comes.   When they him spy
As wild geese that the creeping fowler eye,
Or russet-pated choughs, many in sort,
Rising and cawing at the gun's report,
Sever themselves, and madly sweep the sky,
So, at his sight, away his fellows fly,
And, at our stamp, here o'er and o'er one
        falls ;
He murder cries, and help from Athens calls.
Their sense thus weak, lost with their fears thus
        strong,
More senseless things begin to do them wrong ;
For briers and thorns at their apparel snatch ;
Some, sleeves, — some, hats, — from yielders all
        things catch.
I led them on in this distracted fear,
And left sweet Pyramus translated there :
When in that moment—so it came to pass—
Titania wak'd, and straightway lov'd an ass.
OBE. This falls out better than I could devise. . . .

QUEEN KATHARINE

Page 50

" Although unqueened, yet like
A queen, and daughter to a king."

SHAKESPEARE. "King Henry VIII."

Scene. *The Wood.*

Enter Titania *and* Bottom, *Fairies attending;*
Oberon *behind unseen.*

Tita. Come, sit thee down upon this flowery bed,
    While I thy amiable cheeks do coy,
And stick musk-roses in thy sleek smooth head,
    And kiss thy fair large ears, my gentle joy.

Bot. Where's Pease-blossom?

Peas. Ready.

Bot. Scratch my head, Pease-blossom.—Where's
Monsieur Cobweb?

Cob. Ready.

Bot. Monsieur Cobweb, good monsieur, get your
weapons in your hand, and kill me a red-hipped
humble-bee, on the top of a thistle; and, good
monsieur, bring me the honey-bag. Do not fret
yourself too much in the action, monsieur; and,
good monsieur, have a care the honey-bag break
not; I would be loth to have you overflown
with a honey-bag, signior.—Where's Monsieur
Mustard-seed?

Must. Ready.

Bot. Give me your neif, Monsieur Mustard-seed.
Pray you, leave your courtesy, good monsieur.

Must. What's your will?

Bot. Nothing, good monsieur, but to help Cavalery
Cobweb to scratch. I must to the barber's,
monsieur; for, methinks, I am marvellous hairy

G

about the face ; and I am such a tender ass, if my
hair do but tickle me, I must scratch.

TITA. What, wilt thou hear some music, my sweet
love ?

BOT. I have a reasonable good ear in music ; let's have
the tongs and the bones.

[Music, Tongs, Rural Music.

TITA. Or say, sweet love, what thou desir'st to eat ?

BOT. Truly a peck of provender ; I could munch your
good dry oats. Methinks, I have a great desire
to a bottle of hay ; good hay, sweet hay, hath no
fellow.

TITA. I have a venturous fairy that shall seek
The squirrel's hoard, and fetch thee thence new
nuts.

BOT. I had rather have a handful or two of dried peas.
But, I pray you, let none of your people stir me :
I have an exposition of sleep come upon me.

TITA. Sleep thou, and I will wind thee in my arms.
Fairies, be gone, and be all ways away.

[Exeunt Fairies.

So doth the woodbine the sweet honeysuckle
Gently entwist ; the female ivy so
Enrings the barky fingers of the elm.
O, how I love thee ! how I dote on thee !

[They sleep.

Enter PUCK.

OBERON *[advancing]*. Welcome, good Robin. Seest
thou this sweet sight ?

Her dotage now I do begin to pity:
For, meeting her of late behind the wood,
Seeking sweet favours for this hateful fool,
I did upbraid her, and fall out with her;
For she his hairy temples then had rounded
With coronet of fresh and fragrant flowers;
And that same dew, which sometimes on the buds
Was wont to swell like round and orient pearls,
Stood now within the pretty flowerets' eyes,
Like tears that did their own disgrace bewail.
When I had at my pleasure taunted her,
And she in mild terms begged my patience,
I then did ask of her her changeling child;
Which straight she gave me, and her fairy sent
To bear him to my bower in fairy land.
And now I have the boy, I will undo
This hateful imperfection of her eyes:
And, gentle Puck, take this transformèd scalp
From off the head of this Athenian swain,
That, he awaking when the other do,
May all to Athens back again repair,
And think no more of this night's accidents,
But as the fierce vexation of a dream:—
But first I will release the fairy queen.

SHAKESPEARE.

A Midsummer-Night's Dream.

ROSALIND AND CELIA

IN THE FOREST OF ARDEN

Rosalind, disguised as a man, talks with Celia of Orlando.

ROSALIND. Never talk to me; I will weep.

CELIA. Do, I pr'ythee; but yet have the grace to consider that tears do not become a man.

Ros. But have I not cause to weep?

CEL. As good a cause as one would desire; therefore weep.

Ros. His very hair is of the dissembling colour.

CEL. Something browner than Judas's. Marry, his kisses are Judas's own children.

Ros. I' faith, his hair is of a good colour.

CEL. An excellent colour: your chestnut was ever the only colour.

Ros. And his kissing is as full of sanctity as the touch of holy bread.

CEL. He hath bought a pair of cast lips of Diana: a nun of winter's sisterhood kisses not more religiously; the very ice of chastity is in them.

Ros. But why did he swear he would come this morning, and comes not?

CEL. Nay, certainly, there is no truth in him.

Ros. Do you think so?

CEL. Yes; I think he is not a pick-purse, nor a horse-stealer; but for his verity in love, I do think him as concave as a covered goblet or a worm-eaten nut.

ROS. Not true in love?

CEL. Yes, when he is in; but I think he is not in.

ROS. You have heard him swear downright he was.

CEL. *Was* is not *is*; besides, the oath of a lover is no stronger than the word of a tapster; they are both the confirmers of false reckonings. He attends here in the forest on the duke your father.

ROS. I met the duke yesterday and had much question with him. He asked me of what parentage I was; I told him, of as good as he; so he laughed and let me go. But what talk we of fathers, when there is such a man as Orlando?

CEL. O, that's a brave man! he writes brave verses, speaks brave words, swears brave oaths, and breaks them bravely, quite traverse, athwart the heart of his lover; as a puny tilter that spurs his horse but on one side, breaks his staff like a noble goose. But all's brave that youth mounts and folly guides.

SHAKESPEARE.

As You Like It.

G 2

PERDITA

PERDITA. O Proserpina,
 For the flowers now that, frighted, thou lett'st fall
 From Dis's waggon!—daffodils,
 That come before the swallow dares, and take
 The winds of March with beauty; violets dim,
 But sweeter than the lids of Juno's eyes,
 Or Cytherea's breath; pale primroses,
 That die unmarried ere they can behold
 Bright Phœbus in his strength, a malady
 Most incident to maids; bold oxlips, and
 The crown-imperial; lilies of all kinds,
 The flower-de-luce being one. O, these I lack,
 To make you garlands of, and, my sweet friend,
 To strew him o'er and o'er.
FLORIZEL. What, like a corse?
PERDITA. No, like a bank, for love to lie and play on,
 Not like a corse; or, if,—not to be buried
 But quick, and in mine arms. Come, take your
  flowers.
 Methinks, I play as I have seen them do
 In Whitsun-pastorals: sure, this robe of mine
 Does change my disposition.

FLORIZEL. What you do
    Still betters what is done. When you speak, sweet,
        sweet,
    I 'd have you do it ever: when you sing
    I'd have you buy and sell so; so give alms;
    Pray so; and, for the ordering your affairs,
    To sing them too: when you do dance, I wish you
    A wave o' the sea, that you might ever do
    Nothing but that; move still, still so,
    And own no other function: each your doing,
    So singular in each particular,
    Crowns what you are doing in the present deeds,
    That all your acts are queens.

SHAKESPEARE.

The Winter's Tale.

THE WOOING OF MINNEHAHA

At the doorway of his wigwam
Sat the ancient Arrow-maker,
In the land of the Dacotahs,
Making arrow-heads of jasper,
Arrow-heads of chalcedony.
At his side, in all her beauty,
Sat the lovely Minnehaha,
Sat his daughter, Laughing Water,
Plaiting mats of flags and rushes;
Of the past the old man's thoughts were,
And the maiden's of the future.

     He was thinking, as he sat there,
Of the days when with such arrows
He had struck the deer and bison,
On the Muskoday, the meadow;
Shot the wild geese, flying southward,
On the wing, the clamorous Wawa;
Thinking of the great war parties,
How they came to buy his arrows,   .
Could not fight without his arrows.
Ah, no more such noble warriors
Could be found on earth as they were!
Now the men were all like women,
Only used their tongues for weapons!

She was thinking of a hunter,
From another tribe and country,
Young and tall, and very handsome,
Who one morning, in the Spring-time,
Came to buy her father's arrows,
Sat and rested in the wigwam,
Lingered long about the doorway,
Looking back as he departed.
She had heard her father praise him,
Praise his courage and his wisdom ;
Would he come again for arrows
To the Falls of Minnehaha ?
On the mat her hands lay idle,
And her eyes were very dreamy.

Through their thoughts they heard a
      footstep,
Heard a rustling in the branches,
And with glowing cheek and forehead,
With the deer upon his shoulders,
Suddenly from out the woodlands
Hiawatha stood before them.

Straight the ancient Arrow-maker
Looked up gravely from his labour,
Laid aside the unfinished arrow,
Bade him enter at the doorway,
Saying as he rose to meet him,
' Hiawatha, you are welcome ! '

At the feet of Laughing Water
Hiawatha laid his burden,
Threw the red deer from his shoulders.

And the maiden looked up at him,
Looked up from her mat of rushes,
Said, with gentle look and accent,
'You are welcome, Hiawatha!'
    Very spacious was the wigwam,
Made of deer-skin dressed and whitened,
With the gods of the Dacotahs
Drawn and painted on its curtains,
And so tall the doorway, hardly
Hiawatha stooped to enter,
Hardly touched his eagle feathers
As he entered at the doorway.
    Then uprose the Laughing Water
From the ground, fair Minnehaha
Laid aside her mat unfinished,
Brought forth food and set before them,
Water brought them from the brooklet,
Gave them food in earthen vessels,
Gave them drink in bowls of bass-wood,
Listened while the guest was speaking,
Listened while her father answered,
But not once her lips she opened,
Not a single word she uttered.
    Yes, as in a dream she listened
To the words of Hiawatha,
As he talked of old Nakomis,
Who had nursed him in his childhood,
As he told of his companions,
Chibaibos, the musician,
And the very strong man, Kwasind,

And of happiness and plenty
In the land of the Ojibways,
In the pleasant land and peaceful.
    'After many years of warfare,
Many years of strife and bloodshed,
There is peace between the Ojibways
And the tribe of the Dacotahs.'
Thus continued Hiawatha,
And then added, speaking slowly,
'That this peace may last for ever,
And our hands be clasped more closely,
And our hearts be more united,
Give me as my wife this maiden,
Minnehaha, Laughing Water,
Loveliest of Dacotah women!'
    And the ancient Arrow-maker
Paused a moment ere he answered,
Smoked a little while in silence,
Looked at Hiawatha proudly,
Fondly looked at Laughing Water,
And made answer, very gravely,
'Yes, if Minnehaha wishes.
Let your heart speak, Minnehaha.'
    And the lovely Laughing Water
Seemed more lovely, as she stood there,
Neither willing nor reluctant,
As she went to Hiawatha,
Softly took the seat beside him,
While she said, and blushed to say it,
'I will follow you, my husband!'

This was Hiawatha's wooing!
Thus it was he won the daughter
Of the ancient Arrow-maker,
In the land of the Dacotahs!

HENRY WADSWORTH LONGFELLOW.

Hiawatha.

THE QUEEN'S MARIE

Page 55

" Yestreen the queen had four Maries,
The night she'll hae but three,
There was Marie Seaton, and Marie Beaton,
And Marie Carmichael, and me."

"The Queen's Marie"

HELEN OF KIRKCONNELL

I WISH I were where Helen lies!
Night and day on me she cries;
O that I were where Helen lies,
    On fair Kirkconnell lee!

Curst be the heart that thought the thought,
And curst the hand that fired the shot,
When in my arms burd Helen dropt,
    And died to succour me!

O think ye na my heart was sair,
When my love dropt down and spak nae mair?
There did she swoon wi' meikle care,
    On fair Kirkconnell lee!

As I went down the water-side,
None but my foe to be my guide,
None but my foe to be my guide,
    On fair Kirkconnell lee—

I lighted down, my sword did draw,
I hackèd him in pieces sma',
I hackèd him in pieces sma',
    For her sake that died for me.

H

O Helen fair, beyond compare!
I 'll weave a garland of thy hair,
Shall bind my heart for evermair,
    Until the day I dee!

O that I were where Helen lies!
Night and day on me she cries;
Out of my bed she bids me rise.
    Says, ' Haste, and come to me!'

O Helen fair! O Helen chaste!
Were I with thee I would be blest,
Where thou lies low and takes thy rest,
    On fair Kirkconnell lee.

I wish my grave were growing green;
A winding-sheet drawn o'er my een,
And I in Helen's arms lying,
    On fair Kirkconnell lee.

I wish I were where Helen lies!
Night and day on me she cries,
And I am weary of the skies,
    For her sake that died for me.

                   ANONYMOUS.

THE door of the jail being flung open from within, there appeared, in the first place, like a black shadow emerging into the sunshine, the grim and gristly presence of the town-beadle, with a sword by his side, and his staff of office in his hand. This personage prefigured and represented in his aspect the whole dismal severity of the Puritanic code of law, which it was his business to administer in its final and closest application to the offender. Stretching forth the official staff in his left hand, he laid his right upon the shoulder of a young woman, whom he thus drew forward, until, on the threshold of the prison-door, she repelled him, by an action marked with natural dignity and force of character, and stepped into the open air as if by her own free will. She bore in her arms a child, a baby of some three months old, who winked and turned aside its little face from the too vivid light of day; because its existence, heretofore, had brought it acquaintance only with the grey twilight of a dungeon, or other darksome apartment of the prison.

When the young woman—the mother of this child —stood fully revealed before the crowd, it seemed to be her first impulse to clasp the infant closely to her bosom; not so much by an impulse of motherly affection, as that she might thereby conceal a certain token, which was wrought or fastened into her dress. In a moment, however, wisely judging that one token of her shame would but poorly serve to hide another, she took the baby on her arm, and with a burning blush, and yet a haughty smile, and a glance that would not be abashed, looked around at her towns-people and neighbours.   On the breast of her gown, in fine red cloth, surrounded with an elaborate embroidery and fantastic flourishes of gold thread, appeared the letter A.   It was so artistically done, and with so much fertility and gorgeous luxuriance of fancy, that it had all the effect of a last and fitting decoration to the apparel that she wore, and which was of splendour in accordance with the taste of the age, but greatly beyond what was allowed by the sumptuary regulations of the colony.

The young woman was tall, with a figure of perfect elegance on a large scale.   She had dark and abundant hair, so glossy that it threw off the sunshine with a gleam ; and a face which, besides being beautiful from regularity of feature and richness of complexion, had the impressiveness belonging to a marked brow and deep black eyes. She was ladylike, too, after the manner of the feminine gentility of those days ; characterised by a certain state and dignity, rather than by the delicate, evanescent, and indescribable grace which is now recognised as its indication.   And never had Hester Prynne appeared more ladylike, in the antique interpretation of the term, than as she issued from the prison. Those who had before known her, and had expected to behold her dimmed and obscured by a disastrous cloud, were astonished and even startled to perceive how her beauty shone out, and made a halo of the misfortune and ignominy in which she was enveloped. It may be true that, to a sensitive observer, there was something exquisitely painful in it. Her attire, which, indeed, she had wrought for the occasion in prison, and had modelled much after her own fancy, seemed to express the attitude of her spirit, the desperate recklessness of her mood, by its wild and picturesque peculiarity. But the point which drew all eyes, and, as it were, transfigured the wearer—so that both men and women who had been familiarly acquainted with Hester Prynne were now impressed as if they beheld her for the first time—was the SCARLET LETTER, so fantastically embroidered and illuminated upon her bosom. It had the effect of a spell, taking her out of the ordinary relations with humanity, and enclosing her in a sphere by herself. . . .

A lane was forthwith opened through the crowd of spectators. Preceded by the beadle, and attended by an irregular procession of stern-browed men and unkindly visaged women, Hester Prynne set forth towards the place appointed for her punishment. A crowd of eager and curious schoolboys, understanding little of the matter in hand, except that it gave them a half-holiday, ran before her progress, turning their heads continually to stare into her face and at the

H 2

winking baby in her arms, and at the ignominious letter on her breast. It was no great distance, in those days, from the prison-door to the market-place. Measured by the prisoner's experience, however, it might be reckoned a journey of some length; for haughty as her demeanour was, she perchance underwent an agony from every footstep of those that thronged to see her, as if her heart had been flung into the street for them all to spurn and trample upon. In our nature, however, there is provision, alike marvellous and merciful, that the sufferer should never know the intensity of what he endures by its present torture, but chiefly by the pang that rankles after it. With almost a serene deportment, therefore, Hester Prynne passed through this portion of her ordeal, and came to a sort of scaffold, at the western extremity of the market-place. It stood nearly beneath the eaves of Boston's earliest church, and appeared to be a fixture there.

In fact, this scaffold constituted a portion of a penal machine, which now, for two or three generations past, has been merely historical and traditionary among us, but was held, in the old time, to be as effectual an agent, in the promotion of good citizenship, as ever was the guillotine among the terrorists of France. It was, in short, the platform of the pillory; and above it rose the framework of that instrument of discipline, so fashioned as to confine the human head in its tight grasp, and thus hold it up to the public gaze. The very ideal of ignominy was embodied and made manifest in this contrivance of wood and iron. There can be no outrage, methinks, against our common nature—whatever be the delinquencies of the individual—no outrage more flagrant than to forbid the culprit to hide his face for shame; as it was the essence of this punishment to do. In Hester Prynne's instance, however, as not infrequently in other cases, her sentence bore that she should stand a certain time upon the platform, but without undergoing that gripe about the neck and confinement of the head, the proneness to which was the most devilish character of this ugly engine. Knowing well her part, she ascended a flight of wooden steps, and was thus displayed to the surrounding multitude, at about the height of a man's shoulder above the street.

Had there been a Papist among the crowd of Puritans, he might have seen in this beautiful woman, so picturesque in her attire and mien, and with the infant at her bosom, an object to remind him of the image of Divine Maternity, which so many illustrious painters have vied with one another to represent; something which should remind him, indeed, but only by contrast, of that sacred image of sinless motherhood, whose infant was to redeem the world. Here, there was the taint of deepest sin in the most sacred quality of human life, working such effect, that the world was only the darker for this woman's beauty, and the more lost for the infant she had borne.

NATHANIEL HAWTHORNE.
The Scarlet Letter.

STELLA'S BIRTHDAY

[MARCH 13, 1727.]

THIS day, whate'er the Fates decree,
Shall still be kept with joy by me.
This day, then, let us not be told
That you are sick, and I grown old;
Nor think of our approaching ills,
And talk of spectacles and pills.
To-morrow will be time enough
To hear such mortifying stuff.
Yet, since from reason may be brought
A better and more pleasing thought,
Which can in spite of all decays
Support a few remaining days,
From not the gravest of divines
Accept for once some serious lines.

    Although we now can form no more
Long schemes of life, as heretofore,
Yet you, while time is running fast,
Can look with joy on what is past.
    Were future happiness and pain
A mere contrivance of the brain;
As atheists argue, to entice
And fit their proselytes for vice

(The only comfort they propose,
To have companions in their woes)—
Grant this the case, yet sure 'tis hard
That virtue, styled its own reward,
And by all sages understood
To be the chief of human good,
Should acting die, nor leave behind
Some lasting pleasure in the mind,
Which, by remembrance, will assuage
Grief, sickness, poverty and age;
And strongly shoot a radiant dart
To shine through life's declining part.
    Say, Stella, feel you no content,
Reflecting on a life well spent?
Your skilful hand employed to save
Despairing wretches from the grave,
And then supporting with your store
Those whom you dragged from death before:
So Providence on mortals waits,
Preserving what it first creates.
Your gen'rous boldness to defend
An innocent and absent friend;
That courage which can make you just
To merit humbled in the dust;
The detestation you express
For vice in all its glittering dress;
That patience under tort'ring pain,
When stubborn Stoics would complain;
Must these like empty shadows pass,
Or forms reflected from a glass,

Or mere chimæras in the mind,
That fly, and leave no mark behind?
Does not the body thrive and grow
By food of twenty years ago?
And, had it not been still supplied,
It must a thousand times have died;
Then who with reason can maintain
That no effects of food remain?
And is not virtue in mankind
The nutriment that feeds the mind,
Upheld by each good action past,
And still continued by the last?
Then who with reason can pretend
That all effects of virtue end?

Believe me, Stella, when you show
That true contempt for things below,
Nor prize your life for other ends
Than merely to oblige your friends,
Your former actions claim their part,
And join to fortify your heart:
For Virtue, in her daily race,
Like Janus, bears a double face;
Looks back with joy when she has gone,
And therefore goes with courage on.
She at your sickly couch will wait,
And guide you to a better state.

O then, whatever Heaven intends,
Take pity on your pitying friends!
Nor let your ills affect your mind
To fancy they can be unkind.

Me, surely me, you ought to spare,
Who gladly would your suff'ring share,
Or give my scrap of life to you,
And think it far beneath your due ;
You, to whose care so oft I owe
That I 'm alive to tell you so.

JONATHAN SWIFT.

As they came up to the house at Walcote, the windows from within were lighted up with friendly welcome; the supper-table was spread in the oak-parlour; it seemed as if forgiveness and love were waiting the returning prodigal. Two or three familiar faces of domestics were on the look-out at the porch—the old housekeeper was there, and young Lockwood from Castlewood in my lord's livery of tawny and blue. His dear mistress pressed his arm as they passed into the hall. Her eyes beamed out on him with affection indescribable. 'Welcome!' was all she said, as she looked up, putting back her fair curls and black hood. A sweet rosy smile blushed on her face; Harry thought he had never seen her look so charming. Her face was lighted with a joy that was brighter than beauty; she took a hand of her son who was in the hall waiting his mother; she did not quit Esmond's arm.

'Welcome, Harry!' my young lord echoed after her. 'Here we are all come to say so. Here's old Pincot, hasn't she grown handsome?' and Pincot, who was older and no handsomer than usual, made a curtsey to the Captain, as she called Esmond, and told my lord to 'Have done, now!'

'And here's Jack Lockwood. He'll make a famous

UNA AND THE RED CROSS KNIGHT

Page 66

" A lovely lady rode him fair beside
Upon a lowly ass more white than snow."

SPENSER. "Faery Queen."

grenadier, Jack; and so shall I; we'll both 'list under you, cousin. As soon as I am seventeen, I go to the army—every gentleman goes to the army. Look! who comes here—ho, ho!' he burst into a laugh. ''Tis Mistress Trix with a new ribbon; I knew she would put one on as soon as she heard a captain was coming to supper.'

This laughing colloquy took place in the hall of Walcote House: in the midst of which is a staircase that leads from an open gallery, where are the doors of the sleeping chambers: and from one of these, a wax candle in her hand, and illuminating her, came Mistress Beatrix—the light falling indeed upon the scarlet ribbon which she wore, and upon the most brilliant white neck in the world.

Esmond had left a child and found a woman, grown beyond the common height; and arrived at such dazzling completeness of beauty, that his eyes might well show surprise and delight at beholding her. In hers there was a brightness so lustrous and melting, that I have seen a whole assembly follow her as if by an attraction irresistible: and that night the great Duke was at the playhouse after Ramillies, every soul turned and looked (she chanced to enter at the opposite side of the theatre at the same moment) at her, and not at him. She was a brown beauty: that is, her eyes, hair, and eyebrows and eyelashes were dark: her hair curling with rich undulations, and waving over her shoulders; but her complexion was as dazzling white as snow in sunshine: except her cheeks, which were a bright red, and her lips, which were of a still deeper crimson. Her mouth and chin, they said, were too large and full, and so they might be for a goddess in marble, but not for a woman whose eyes were fire, whose look was love, whose voice was the sweetest low song, whose shape was perfect symmetry, health, decision, activity, whose foot as it planted itself on the ground was firm but flexible, and whose motion, whether rapid or slow, was always perfect grace—agile as a nymph, lofty as a queen—now melting, now imperious, now sarcastic—there was no single movement of hers but was beautiful. As he thinks of her, he who writes feels young again, and remembers a paragon.

So she came holding her dress with one fair rounded arm, and her taper before her, tripping down the stair to meet Esmond.

'She hath put on her scarlet stockings and white shoes,' says my lord, still laughing. 'Oh my fine mistress! is this the way you set your cap at the Captain?' She approached, shining smiles upon Esmond, who could look at nothing but her eyes. She advanced holding forward her head, as if she would have him kiss her as he used to when she was a child.

'Stop,' she said, 'I am grown too big! Welcome, Cousin Harry!' and she made him an arch curtsey, sweeping down to the ground almost, with the most gracious bend, looking up the while with the brightest eyes and sweetest smile. Love seemed to radiate

from her.   Harry eyed her with such a rapture as the
first lover is described as having by Milton.

'*N'est-ce pas ?*' says my lady, in a low, sweet voice,
still hanging on his arm.

Esmond turned round with a start and a blush, as
he met his mistress' clear eyes.   He had forgotten
her, rapt in admiration of the *filia pulcrior.*

'Right foot forward, toe turned out, so ; now drop
the curtsey, and show the red stockings, Trix.   They 've
silver clocks, Harry.   The Dowager sent 'em.   She
went to put 'em on,' cries my lord.

'Hush, you stupid child !' says Miss, smothering
her brother with kisses ; and then she must come and
kiss her mamma, looking all the while at Harry, over
his mistress' shoulder.   And if she did not kiss him,
she gave him both her hands, and then took one of
his in both hands, and said, ' Oh, Harry, we 're so, *so*
glad you 're come !'

W. M. THACKERAY.

Esmond.

THE LAMENT OF FLORA MACDONALD

Far over yon hills of the heather so green,
 And down by the corrie that sings to the sea,
The bonnie young Flora sat sighing her lane,
 The dew on her plaid, and the tear in her e'e.
She looked at a boat which the breezes had swung
 Away on the wave, like a bird of the main ;
And aye as it lessened, she sighed and she sung,
 ' Farewell to the lad I shall ne'er see again !
Farewell to my hero, the gallant and young !
 Farewell to the lad I shall ne'er see again !

' The muircock that crows on the top of Ben Connal,
 He kens o' his bed in a sweet mossy hame ;
The eagle that soars o'er the cliffs of Clan Ronald,
 Unawed and unhunted, his eiry can claim ;
The solan can sleep on his shelve of the shore ;
 The cormorant roost on his rock of the sea :
But, oh ! there is ane whose hard fate I deplore ;
 Nor house, ha', nor hame, in his country has he.
The conflict is past, and our name is no more :
 There's nought left but sorrow for Scotland and
  me.

'The target is torn from the arm of the just,
    The helmet is cleft on the brow of the brave,
The claymore for ever in darkness must rust,
    But red is the sword of the stranger and slave ;
The hoof of the horse, and the foot of the proud,
    Have trode o'er the plumes in the bonnet of blue;
Why slept the red bolt in the breast of the cloud,
    When tyranny revelled in blood of the true ?
Farewell, my young hero, the gallant and good !
    The crown of thy fathers is torn from thy brow.'

JAMES HOGG.

JEANIE AND EFFIE DEANS

THE careful father was absent in his well-stocked byre, foddering those useful and patient animals on whose produce his living depended, and the summer evening was beginning to close in, when Jeanie Deans began to be very anxious for the appearance of her sister, and to fear that she would not reach home before her father returned from the labour of the evening, when it was his custom to have 'family exercise,' and when she knew that Effie's absence would give him the most serious displeasure. These apprehensions hung heavier upon her mind, because, for several preceding evenings, Effie had disappeared about the same time, and her stay, at first so brief as scarce to be noticed, had been gradually protracted to half an hour, and an hour, and on the present occasion had considerably exceeded even this last limit. And now, Jeanie stood at the door, her hands before her eyes to avoid the rays of the level sun, and looked alternately along the various tracks which led towards their dwelling, to see if she could descry the nymph-like form of her sister. There was a wall and a stile which separated the royal domain, or King's Park, as it is called, from the public road; to this pass she frequently directed her attention, when she saw two persons appear there somewhat suddenly, as if they had walked close by the side of the wall to screen themselves from observation. One of them, a man, drew back hastily; the other, a female, crossed the stile, and advanced towards her—it was Effie. She met her sister with that affected liveliness of manner, which, in her rank, and sometimes in those above it, females occasionally assume to hide surprise or confusion; and she carolled as she came—

> ' *The elfin knight sat on the brae,*
> *The broom grows bonny, the broom grows fair ;*
> *And by there came lilting a lady so gay,*
> *And we daurna gang down to the broom nae mair.*'

'Whisht, Effie,' said her sister; 'our father's coming out o' the byre——' The damsel stinted her song.— 'Whare hae ye been sae late at e'en ?'

'It's no late, lass,' answered Effie.

'It's chappit eight on every clock o' the town, and the sun's gaun down ahint the Corstorphine hills.— Whare can ye hae been sae late ?'

'Nae gate,' answered Effie.

'And wha was that parted wi' you at the stile ?'

'Naebody,' replied Effie, once more.

'Nae gate ?—Naebody ?—I wish it may be a right gate, and a right body, that keeps folks out sae late at e'en, Effie.'

'What needs ye be aye speering then at folk ?' retorted Effie. 'I'm sure, if ye'll ask nae questions, I'll tell ye nae lees. I never ask what brings the

Laird of Dumbiedikes glowering here like a wull-cat (only he's e'en greener and no sae gleg) day after day, till we are a' like to gaunt our chafts aff.'

'Because ye ken very weel he comes to see our father,' said Jeanie, in answer to this pert remark.

'And Dominie Butler—Does he come to see our father, that's sae taen wi' his Latin words?' said Effie, delighted to find that, by carrying the war into the enemy's country, she could divert the threatened attack upon herself, and with the petulance of youth she pursued her triumph over her prudent elder sister. She looked at her with a sly air, in which there was something like irony, as she chanted in a low but marked tone, a scrap of an old Scotch song—

> *Through the kirkyard*
> *I met wi' the laird,*
> *The silly puir body he said me nae harm ;*
> *But just ere 'twas dark,*
> *I met wi' the clerk——'*

Here the songstress stopped, looked full at her sister, and, observing the tears gather in her dark eyes, she suddenly flung her arms round her neck, and kissed them away. Jeanie, though hurt and displeased, was unable to resist the caresses of this untaught child of nature, whose good and evil seemed to flow rather from impulse than from reflection. But as she returned the sisterly kiss, in token of perfect reconciliation, she could not suppress the gentle reproof—'Effie, if ye will learn fule sangs, ye might make a kinder use of them.'

'And so I might, Jeanie,' continued the girl, clinging to her sister's neck; 'and I wish I had never learned ane o' them—and I wish we had never come here—and I wish my tongue had been blistered or I had vexed ye.'

'Never mind that, Effie,' replied the affectionate sister; 'I canna be muckle vexed wi' onything ye say to me—but oh, dinna vex our father!'

'I will not—I will not,' replied Effie; 'and if there were as mony dances the morn's night as there are merry dancers in the north firmament on a frosty e'en, I winna budge an inch to gang near ane o' them.'

. . . .

Jeanie parted from her sister, with a mixed feeling of regret, apprehension, and hope. She could not be so confident concerning Effie's prudence as her father, for she had observed her more narrowly, had more sympathy with her feelings, and could better estimate the temptations to which she was exposed. On the other hand, Mrs. Saddletree was an observing, shrewd, notable woman, entitled to exercise over Effie the full authority of a mistress, and likely to do so strictly, yet with kindness. Her removal to Saddletree's, it was most probable, would also serve to break off some idle acquaintances, which Jeanie suspected her sister to have formed in the neighbouring suburb. Upon the whole, then, she viewed her departure from Saint Leonard's with pleasure, and it was not until the very moment of their parting for the first time in their lives, that she felt the full force of sisterly sorrow. While they repeatedly kissed each other's cheeks and wrung each other's hands, Jeanie took that moment of affectionate sympathy, to press upon her sister the necessity of the utmost caution in her conduct whilst residing in Edinburgh. Effie listened, without once raising her large dark eyelashes, from which the drops fell so fast as almost to resemble a fountain. At the conclusion she sobbed again, kissed her sister, promised to recollect all the good counsel she had given her, and they parted.

SIR WALTER SCOTT.

The Heart of Midlothian.

SOPHIA, then, the only daughter of Mr. Western, was a middle-sized woman, but rather inclining to tall. Her shape was not only exact, but extremely delicate, and the nice proportion of her arms promised the truest symmetry in her limbs. Her hair, which was black, was so luxuriant that it reached her middle, before she cut it to comply with the modern fashion; and it was now curled so gracefully in her neck, that few could believe it to be her own. If envy could find any part of the face which demanded less commendation than the rest, it might possibly think her forehead might have been higher without prejudice to her. Her eyebrows were full, even, and arched beyond the power of art to imitate. Her black eyes had a lustre in them which all her softness could not extinguish. Her nose was exactly regular; and her mouth, in which were two rows of ivory, exactly answered Sir John Suckling's description in those lines:

> *' Her lips were red, and one was thin,*
> *Compar'd to that was next her chin,*
> *Some bee had stung it newly.'*

Her cheeks were of the oval kind; and in her right she had a dimple, which the least smile discovered. Her chin had certainly its share in forming the beauty of her face; but it was difficult to say it was either large or small, though perhaps it was rather of the former kind. Her complexion had rather more of the lily than the rose; but when exercise or modesty increased her natural colour, no vermilion could equal it. Then one might cry out, with the celebrated Dr. Donne:

> '*Her pure and eloquent blood*
> *Spoke in her cheeks, and so distinctly wrought,*
> *That one might almost say her body thought.*'

Her neck was long and finely turned: and here, if I was not afraid of offending her delicacy, I might justly say, the highest beauties of the famous *Venus de Medicis* were outdone. Here was whiteness which no lilies, ivory, or alabaster could match. The finest cambric might indeed be supposed from envy to cover that bosom which was so much whiter than itself. It was indeed

> '*Nitor splendens Pario marmore purius.*'

'A gloss shining beyond the purest brightness of Parian marble.'

Such was the outside of Sophia; nor was this beautiful frame disgraced by an inhabitant unworthy of it. Her mind was every way equal to her person; nay, the latter borrowed some charms from the former; for when she smiled, the sweetness of her temper diffused the glory over her countenance which no regularity of features can give. . . .

It may, however, be proper to say that, whatever

BOTTOM AND TITANIA

Page 68

TITANIA. *Come, sit thee down upon this flowery bed,*
While I thy amiable cheeks do coy,
And stick mush-roses in thy sleek smooth head.

SHAKESPEARE. "A Midsummer Night's Dream."

mental accomplishments she had derived from nature, they were somewhat improved and cultivated by art: for she had been educated under the care of an aunt, who was a lady of great discretion, and was thoroughly acquainted with the world, having lived in her youth about the court, whence she had retired some years since into the country. By her conversations and instructions, Sophia was perfectly well-bred, though perhaps she wanted a little of that ease in her behaviour which is to be acquired only by habit, and living within what is called the polite circle. But this, to say the truth, is often too dearly purchased; and though it hath charms so inexpressible, that the French, perhaps, among other qualities, mean to express this when they declare they know not what it is; yet its absence is well compensated by innocence, nor can good sense and a natural gentility ever stand in need of it.

HENRY FIELDING.

Tom Jones.

FIELDING'S 'AMELIA'

VIRTUES and woes alike too great for man
    In the soft tale oft claim the useless sigh ;
For vain the attempt to realise the plan,
    On Folly's wings must imitation fly.
With other aim has Fielding here display'd
    Each social duty and each social care ;
With just yet vivid colouring portray'd
    What every wife should be, what many are.
And sure the parent of a race so sweet
    With double pleasure on the page shall dwell,
Each scene with sympathising breast shall meet,
    While Reason still with smiles delights to tell
Maternal hope, that her loved progeny
In all but sorrows shall Amelias be !

SAMUEL TAYLOR COLERIDGE.

TO MRS. THRALE

ON HER COMPLETING HER THIRTY-FIFTH YEAR

OFT in danger, yet alive,
We have come to thirty-five;
Long may better years arrive,
Better years than thirty-five.
Could philosophers contrive
Life to stop at thirty-five,
Time his hours would never drive
O'er the bounds of thirty-five.
High to soar, and deep to dive,
Nature gives at thirty-five.
Ladies, stock and tend your hive,
Trifle not at thirty-five;
For howe'er we boast and strive,
Life declines from thirty-five;
He that ever hopes to thrive
Must begin at thirty-five;
And all who wisely wish to wive
Must look on Thrale at thirty-five.

SAMUEL JOHNSON.

OLIVIA

(On the eve of her elopement with Squire Thornhill.)

As I only studied my child's real happiness, the
assiduity of Mr. Williams pleased me, as he was in
easy circumstances, prudent, and sincere. It required
but very little encouragement to revive his former
passion; so that in an evening or two he and Mr.
Thornhill met at our house, and surveyed each other
for some time with looks of anger: but Williams owed
his landlord no rent, and little regarded his indigna-
tion. Olivia, on her side, acted the coquet to per-
fection, if that might be called acting which was her
real character, pretending to lavish all her tenderness
on her new lover. Mr. Thornhill appeared quite
dejected at this preference, and, with a pensive air,
took leave; though I own it puzzled me to find him
in so much pain as he appeared to be, when he had it
in his power so easily to remove the cause, by declaring
an honourable passion. But whatever uneasiness he
seemed to endure, it could easily be perceived that
Olivia's anguish was much greater. After any of these
interviews between her lovers, of which there were
several, she usually retired to solitude, and there
indulged her grief. It was in such a situation I found
her one evening, after she had been for some time
supporting a fictitious gaiety.

'You now see, my child,' said I, 'that your confidence in Mr. Thornhill's passion was all a dream; he permits the rivalry of another, every way his inferior, though he knows it lies in his power to secure you to himself by a candid declaration——'

'Yes, papa,' returned she, 'but he has his reasons for this delay, I know he has. The sincerity of his looks and words convinces me of his real esteem. A short time, I hope, will discover the generosity of his sentiments, and convince you that my opinion of him has been more just than yours.'

'Olivia, my darling,' returned I, 'every scheme that has been hitherto pursued to compel him to a declaration has been proposed and planned by yourself, nor can you in the least say that I have constrained you. But you must not suppose, my dear, that I will ever be instrumental in suffering his honest rival to be the dupe of your ill-placed passion. Whatever time you require to bring your fancied admirer to an explanation, shall be granted; but at the expiration of that term, if he is still regardless, I must absolutely insist that honest Mr. Williams shall be rewarded for his fidelity. The character which I have hitherto supported in life demands this from me; and my tenderness as a parent shall never influence my integrity as a man. Name, then, your day; let it be as distant as you think proper, and in the meantime take care to let Mr. Thornhill know the exact time on which I design delivering you up to another. If he really loves you, his own good sense will readily

K 2

suggest that there is but one method alone to prevent his losing you for ever.'

This proposal, which she could not avoid considering as perfectly just, was readily agreed to. She again renewed her most positive promise of marrying Mr. Williams, in case of the other's insensibility; and at the next opportunity, in Mr. Thornhill's presence, that day month was fixed upon for her nuptials with his rival.

Such vigorous proceedings seemed to redouble Mr. Thornhill's anxiety: but what Olivia really felt gave me some uneasiness. In this struggle between prudence and passion, her vivacity quite forsook her, and every opportunity of solitude was sought, and spent in tears. One week passed away; but Mr. Thornhill made no efforts to restrain her nuptials. The succeeding week he was still assiduous, but not more open. On the third he discontinued his visits entirely; and instead of my daughter testifying any impatience, as I expected, she seemed to retain a pensive tranquillity, which I looked upon as resignation. For my own part, I was now sincerely pleased with thinking that my child was going to be secured in a continuance of competence and peace, and frequently applauded her resolution, in preferring happiness to ostentation.

OLIVER GOLDSMITH.
The Vicar of Wakefield.

WE are to go this evening to a private ball, given by Mrs. Stanley, a very fashionable lady of Mrs. Mirvan's acquaintance.

We have been *a-shopping*, as Mrs. Mirvan calls it, all this morning, to buy silks, caps, gauzes, and so forth.

The shops are really very entertaining, especially the mercers; there seem to be six or seven men belonging to each shop; and every one took care, by bowing and smirking, to be noticed. We were conducted from one to another and carried from room to room with so much ceremony, that at first I was almost afraid to go on.

I thought I should never have chosen a silk: for they produced so many, I knew not which to fix upon; and they recommended them all so strongly, that I fancy they thought I only wanted persuasion to buy every thing they showed me. And, indeed, they took so much trouble, that I was almost ashamed I could not.

At the milliners, the ladies we met were so much dressed, that I should rather have imagined they were making visits than purchases. But what most diverted me was, that we were more frequently served by men than women; and such men! so finical, so affected! they seemed to understand every part of a woman's dress better than we do ourselves; and they recommended caps and ribbands with an air of so much importance, that I wished to ask them how long they had left off wearing them.

The dispatch with which they work in these great shops is amazing, for they have promised me a complete suit of linen against the evening.

I have just had my hair dressed. You can't think how oddly my head feels; full of powder and black pins, and a great cushion on the top of it. I believe you would hardly know me, for my face looks quite different to what it did before my hair was dressed. When I shall be able to make use of a comb for myself I cannot tell; for my hair is so much entangled, *frizzled* they call it, that I fear it will be very difficult.

I am half afraid of this ball to-night; for, you know, I have never danced but at school: however, Miss Mirvan says there is nothing in it. . . .

At the Ball.

And very soon after, another gentleman, who seemed about six-and-twenty years old, gaily but not foppishly dressed, and indeed extremely handsome, with an air of mixed politeness and gallantry, desired to know if I was engaged, or would honour him with my hand. So he was pleased to say, though I am sure I know not what honour he could receive from me; but these sort of expressions, I find, are used as words of course, without any distinction of persons, or study of propriety.

Well, I bowed, and I am sure I coloured; for indeed I was frightened at the thoughts of dancing before so many people, all strangers, and, which was worse, *with* a stranger: however, that was unavoidable; for, though I looked round the room several times, I could not see one person that I knew. And so he took my hand, and led me to join in the dance.

The minuets were over before we arrived, for we were kept late by the milliners making us wait for our things.

He seemed very desirous of entering into conversation with me ; but I was seized with such a panic, that I could hardly speak a word, and nothing but the shame of so soon changing my mind prevented my returning to my seat and declining to dance at all.

He appeared to be surprised at my terror, which I believe was but too apparent : however, he asked no questions, though I fear he must think it very strange, for I did not choose to tell him it was owing to my never before dancing but with a school-girl.

His conversation was sensible and spirited; his air and address were open and noble; his manners gentle, attentive, and infinitely engaging; his person is all elegance, and his countenance the most animated and expressive I have ever seen.

In a short time we were joined by Miss Mirvan, who stood next couple to us. But how was I startled when she whispered me that my partner was a nobleman! This gave me a new alarm: how will he be provoked, thought I, when he finds what a simple rustic he has honoured with his choice! one whose ignorance of the world makes her perpetually fear doing something wrong!

That he should be so much my superior every way, quite disconcerted me; and you will suppose my spirits were not much raised, when I heard a lady, in passing us, say, 'This is the most difficult dance I ever saw.'

'O dear, then,' cried Martha to her partner, 'with your leave, I'll sit down till the next.'

'So will I too, then,' cried I, 'for I am sure I can hardly stand.'

'But you must speak to your partner first,' answered she; for he had turned aside to talk with some gentleman. However, I had not sufficient courage to address him; and so away we all three tript, and seated ourselves at another end of the room.

But, unfortunately for me, Miss Mirvan soon after suffered herself to be prevailed upon to attempt the dance; and just as she rose to go, she cried, 'My dear, yonder is your partner, Lord Orville, walking about the room in search of you.'

'Don't leave me then, dear girl!' cried I; but she was obliged to go. And now I was more uneasy than ever; I would have given the world to have seen Mrs. Mirvan, and begged of her to make my apologies; for what, thought I, can I possibly say to him in excuse for running away? He must either conclude me a fool, or half mad; for any one brought up in the

great world, and accustomed to its ways, can have no
idea of such sort of fears as mine.

My confusion increased when I observed that he
was everywhere seeking me, with apparent perplexity
and surprise; but when, at last, I saw him move
towards the place where I sat, I was ready to sink
with shame and distress. I found it absolutely im-
possible to keep my seat, because I could not think
of a word to say for myself; and so I rose, and walked
hastily towards the card-room, resolving to stay with
Mrs. Mirvan the rest of the evening, and not to dance
at all. But before I could find her, Lord Orville saw
and approached me.

He begged to know if I was not well? You may
easily imagine how much I was embarrassed. I made
no answer but hung my head like a fool, and looked
on my fan.

He then, with an air the most respectfully
serious, asked if he had been so unhappy as to offend
me?

'No, indeed!' cried I, and, in hopes of changing
the discourse, and preventing his further inquiries, I
desired to know if he had seen the young lady who
had been conversing with me?

No;—but would I honour him with any commands
to her?

'O, by no means!'

Was there any other person with whom I wished
to speak?

I said *no* before I knew I had answered at all.

Should he have the pleasure of bringing me any refreshment.

I bowed, almost involuntarily.   And away he flew.

I was quite ashamed of being so troublesome, and so much *above* myself as these seeming airs made me appear; but indeed I was too much confused to think or act with any consistency.

If he had not been as swift as lightning, I don't know whether I should not have stolen away again; but he returned in a moment.   When I had drank a glass of lemonade, he hoped, he said, that I would again honour him with my hand, as a new dance was just begun.   I had not the presence of mind to say a single word, and so I let him once more lead me to the place I had left.

FANNY BURNEY.

Evelina.

ROSALIND AND CELIA

Page 76

ROSALIND. *Never talk to me: I will weep.*
CELIA. *Do, I pr'ythee; but yet have the grace to
consider that tears do not become a man. . . . .
Who comes here?*

SHAKESPEARE. "As You Like it."

TO MARY UNWIN

MARY! I want a lyre with other strings,
    Such aid from Heaven as some have feigned they
        drew,
    An eloquence scarce given to mortals, new
And undebased by praise of meaner things,
That, ere through age or woe I shed my wings,
    I may record thy worth with honour due,
    In verse as musical as thou art true,
And that immortalizes whom it sings.
But thou hast little need.   There is a book
    By seraphs writ with beams of heavenly light,
On which the eyes of God not rarely look,
    A chronicle of actions just and bright:
There all thy deeds, my faithful Mary, shine,
And, since thou own'st that praise, I spare thee mine.

WILLIAM COWPER.

ON THE RECEIPT OF MY MOTHER'S
PICTURE OUT OF NORFOLK

Oh that those lips had language!   Life has passed
With me but roughly since I heard thee last.
Those lips are thine—thy own sweet smile I see,
The same that oft in childhood solaced me;
Voice only fails, else how distinct they say,
'Grieve not, my child, chase all thy fears away!'
The meek intelligence of those dear eyes
(Blessed be the art that can immortalize,
The art that baffles Time's tyrannic claim
To quench it) here shines on me still the same.
   Faithful remembrancer of one so dear,
O welcome guest, thou unexpected here!
Who bidst me honour with an artless song,
Affectionate, a mother lost so long.
I will obey, not willingly alone,
But gladly, as the precept were her own:
And, while that face renews my filial grief,
Fancy shall weave a charm for my relief,
Shall steep me in Elysian reverie,
A momentary dream that thou art she.
   My mother! when I learnt that thou wast dead,
Say, wast thou conscious of the tears I shed?
Hover'd thy spirit o'er thy sorrowing son,
Wretch even then, life's journey just begun?

Perhaps thou gavest me, though unfelt, a kiss :
Perhaps a tear, if souls can weep in bliss—
Ah, that maternal smile! It answers—Yes.
I heard the bell toll on thy burial day,
I saw the hearse that bore thee slow away,
And, turning from my nursery window, drew
A long, long sigh, and wept a last adieu!
But was it such ?—It was.—Where thou art gone
Adieus and farewells are a sound unknown.
May I but meet thee on that peaceful shore,
The parting word shall pass my lips no more!
Thy maidens, grieved themselves at my concern,
Oft gave me promise of thy quick return.
What ardently I wished I long believed,
And, disappointed still, was still deceived.
By expectation every day beguiled,
Dupe of *to-morrow* even from a child.
Thus many a sad to-morrow came and went,
Till, all my stock of infant sorrow spent,
I learnt at last submission to my lot ;
But, though I less deplored thee, ne'er forgot.
　　Where once we dwelt our name is heard no
　　　　more,
Children not thine have trod my nursery floor ;
And where the gardener Robin, day by day,
Drew me to school along the public way,
Delighted with my bauble coach, and wrapped
In scarlet mantle warm, and velvet capped,
'Tis now become a history little known,
That once we called the pastoral house our own.

Short-lived possession! but the record fair
That memory keeps, of all thy kindness there,
Still outlives many a storm that has effaced
A thousand other themes less deeply traced.
Thy nightly visits to my chamber made,
That thou mightst know me safe and warmly laid ;
Thy morning bounties ere I left my home,
The biscuit, or confectionary plum ;
The fragrant waters on my cheek bestowed
By thy own hand, till fresh they shone and glowed ;
All this, and more endearing still than all,
Thy constant flow of love, that knew no fall,
Ne'er roughened by those cataracts and brakes
That humour interposed too often makes ;
All this still legible in memory's page,
And still to be so till my latest age,
Adds joy to duty, makes me glad to pay
Such honours to thee as my numbers may :
Perhaps a frail memorial, but sincere,
Not scorned in heaven, though little noticed here.
　　　Could Time, his flight reversed, restore the hours,
When, playing with thy vesture's tissued flowers,
The violet, the pink, and jessamine,
I pricked them into paper with a pin
(And thou wast happier than myself the while,
Wouldst softly speak, and stroke my head and smile),
Could these few pleasant days again appear,
Might one wish bring them, would I wish them here ?
I would not trust my heart—the dear delight
Seems so to be desired, perhaps I might.—

But no—what here we call our life is such
So little to be loved, and thou so much,
That I should ill requite thee to constrain
Thy unbound spirit into bonds again.
    Thou, as a gallant bark from Albion's coast
(The storms all weathered and the oceans crossed)
Shoots into port at some well-havened isle,
Where spices breathe, and brighter seasons smile,
There sits quiescent on the floods that show
Her beauteous form reflected clear below,
While airs impregnated with incense play
Around her, fanning light her streamers gay :
So thou, with sails how swift! hast reached the shore,
'Where tempests never beat nor billows roar,'
And thy loved consort on the dangerous tide
Of life long since has anchored by thy side.
But me, scarce hoping to attain that rest,
Always from port withheld, always distressed—
The howling blasts drive devious, tempest tost,
Sails ripped, seams opening wide, and compass lost,
And day by day some current's thwarting force
Sets me more distant from a prosperous course.
Yet, oh the thought that thou art safe, and he !
That thought is joy, arrive what may to me.
My boast is not, that I deduce my birth
From loins enthroned and rulers of the earth ;
But higher far my proud pretensions rise—
The son of parents passed into the skies !
And now, farewell!—Time unrevoked has run
His wonted course, yet what I wished is done.
    L 2

By contemplation's help, not sought in vain,
I seemed to have lived my childhood o'er again;
To have renewed the joys that once were mine,
Without the sin of violating thine :
And, while the wings of Fancy still are free,
And I can view this mimic show of thee,
Time has but half succeeded in his theft—
Thyself removed, thy power to soothe me left.

WILLIAM COWPER.

MRS. MALAPROP

SCENE. *Dressing-room in* MRS. MALAPROP's *lodging.*
LYDIA LANGUISH *seated on sofa.*

Enter MRS. MALAPROP *and* SIR ANTHONY ABSOLUTE.

MRS. MAL. There, Sir Anthony, there sits the deliberate simpleton who wants to disgrace her family, and lavish herself on a fellow not worth a shilling.

LYD. Madam. I thought you once—

MRS. MAL. You thought, miss! I don't know any business you have to think at all—thought does not become a young woman. But the point we would request of you is, that you will promise to forget this fellow—to illiterate him, I say, quite from your memory.

LYD. Ah, madam! our memories are independent of our wills. It is not so easy to forget.

MRS. MAL. But I say it is, miss; there is nothing on earth so easy as to forget, if a person chooses to set about it. I'm sure I have as much forgot your poor dear uncle as if he had never existed —and I thought it my duty so to do; and let me tell you, Lydia, these violent memories don't become a young woman.

SIR ANTH. Why sure she won't pretend to remember what she's ordered not!—ay, this comes of her reading!

LYD. What crime, madam, have I committed to be treated thus?

MRS. MAL. Now don't attempt to extirpate yourself from the matter; you know I have proof controvertible of it.—But tell me, will you promise to do as you're bid? Will you take a husband of your friends' choosing?

LYD. Madam, I must tell you plainly, that had I no preferment for any one else, the choice you have made would be my aversion.

MRS. MAL. What business have you, miss, with preference and aversion? They don't become a young woman; and you ought to know, that as both always wear off, 'tis safest in matrimony to begin with a little aversion. I'm sure I hated your poor dear uncle before marriage as if he'd been a blackamoor—and yet, miss, you are sensible what a wife I made!—and when it pleased Heaven to release me from him, 'tis unknown what tears I shed!—But suppose we were going to give you another choice, will you promise us to give up this Beverley?

LYD. Could I belie my thoughts so far as to give that promise, my actions would certainly as far belie my words.

MRS. MAL. Take yourself to your room. You are fit company for nothing but your own ill-humours.

LYD. Willingly, ma'am — I cannot change for the worse. [*Exit.*

MRS. MAL. There's a little intricate hussy for you!

SIR ANTH. It is not to be wondered at, ma'am—all this is the natural consequence of teaching girls to read. Had I a thousand daughters, by Heaven! I'd as soon have them taught the black art as their alphabet!

MRS. MAL. Nay, nay, Sir Anthony, you are an absolute misanthropy.

SIR ANTH. In my way hither, Mrs. Malaprop, I observed your niece's maid coming forth from a circulating library!—She had a book in each hand —they were half-bound volumes with marble covers!—From that moment I guessed how full of duty I should see her mistress!

MRS. MAL. Those are vile places, indeed!

SIR ANTH. Madam, a circulating library in a town is as an ever-green tree of diabolical knowledge! It blossoms through the year!—And depend upon it, Mrs. Malaprop, that they who are so fond of handling the leaves, will long for the fruit at last.

MRS. MAL. Fy, fy, Sir Anthony! you surely speak laconically.

SIR ANTH. Why, Mrs. Malaprop, in moderation now, what would you have a woman know?

MRS. MAL. Observe me, Sir Anthony.—I would by no means wish a daughter of mine to be a progeny of learning; I don't think so much learning becomes a young woman; for instance,

I would never let her meddle with Greek, or Hebrew, or algebra, or simony, or fluxions, or paradoxes, or such inflammatory branches of learning—neither would it be necessary for her to handle any of your mathematical, astronomical, diabolical instruments. — But, Sir Anthony, I would send her, at nine years old, to a boarding-school, in order to learn a little ingenuity and artifice. Then, sir, she should have a supercilious knowledge in accounts; and as she grew up, I would have her instructed in geometry, that she might know something of the contagious countries; but above all, Sir Anthony, she should be mistress of orthodoxy, that she might not mis-spell, and mispronounce words so shamefully as girls usually do; and likewise that she might reprehend the true meaning of what she is saying. This, Sir Anthony, is what I would have a woman know; and I don't think there is a superstitious article in it.

RICHARD BRINSLEY SHERIDAN.

The Rivals.

TO MARY IN HEAVEN

THOU ling'ring star, with less'ning ray,
    That lov'st to greet the early morn,
Again thou usher'st in the day
    My Mary from my soul was torn.
O Mary! dear departed shade!
    Where is thy place of blissful rest?
See'st thou thy lover lowly laid?
    Hear'st thou the groans that rend his breast?

That sacred hour can I forget,
    Can I forget the hallow'd grove,
Where, by the winding Ayr, we met,
    To live one day of parting love!
Eternity cannot efface
    Those records dear of transports past;
Thy image at our last embrace;
    Ah! little thought we 'twas our last!

Ayr, gurgling, kiss'd his pebbled shore,
    O'erhung with wild woods, thick'ning green;
The fragrant birch and hawthorn hoar,
    Twined am'rous round the raptur'd scene:
The flowers sprang wanton to be prest,
    The birds sang love on every spray—
Till too, too soon the glowing west
    Proclaim'd the speed of wingèd day.

Still o'er these scenes my mem'ry wakes,
 And fondly broods with miser-care!
Time but th' impression stronger makes,
 As streams their channels deeper wear.
My Mary! dear departed shade!
 Where is thy place of blissful rest?
See'st thou thy lover lowly laid?
 Hear'st thou the groans that rend his breast?

ROBERT BURNS.

GUINEVERE

Page 11

" Her memory from old habit of the mind
Went slipping back upon the golden days
In which she saw him first, when Launcelot came."

TENNYSON. "Guinevere."

ELIZABETH BENNET

~

ELIZABETH BENNET had been obliged, by the scarcity of gentlemen, to sit down for two dances; and during part of that time, Mr. Darcy had been standing near enough for her to overhear a conversation between him and Mr. Bingley, who came from the dance for a few minutes to press his friend to join it.

'Come, Darcy,' said he, 'I must have you dance. I hate to see you standing about by yourself in this stupid manner. You had much better dance.'

'I certainly shall not. You know how I detest it, unless I am particularly acquainted with my partner. At such an assembly as this, it would be insupportable. Your sisters are engaged, and there is not another woman in the room whom it would not be a punishment to me to stand up with.'

'I would not be so fastidious as you are,' cried Bingley, 'for a kingdom! Upon my honour, I never met with so many pleasant girls in my life as I have this evening; and there are several of them, you see, uncommonly pretty.'

'*You* are dancing with the only handsome girl in the room,' said Mr. Darcy, looking at the eldest Miss Bennet.

M

'Oh, she is the most beautiful creature I ever beheld! But there is one of her sisters sitting down just behind you, who is very pretty, and I daresay very agreeable. Do let me ask my partner to introduce you.'

'Which do you mean?' and turning round, he looked for a moment at Elizabeth, till, catching her eye, he withdrew his own, and coldly said, 'She is tolerable; but not handsome enough to tempt *me*; and I am in no humour at present to give consequence to young ladies who are slighted by other men. You had better return to your partner and enjoy her smiles, for you are wasting your time with me.'

Mr. Bingley followed his advice. Mr. Darcy walked off; and Elizabeth remained with no very cordial feelings towards him. She told the story, however, with great spirit among her friends; for she had a lively, playful disposition, which delighted in anything ridiculous.

II

Occupied in observing Mr. Bingley's attentions to her sister, Elizabeth was far from suspecting that she was herself becoming an object of some interest in the eyes of his friend. Mr. Darcy had at first scarcely allowed her to be pretty: he had looked at her without admiration at the ball; and when they next met, he looked at her only to criticise. But no sooner had he made it clear to himself and his friends that she had hardly a good feature in her face, than he began to find it rendered uncommonly intelligent by the beautiful expression of her dark eyes. To this discovery succeeded some others equally mortifying. Though he had detected with a critical eye more than one failure of perfect symmetry in her form, he was forced to acknowledge her figure to be light and pleasing; and in spite of his asserting that her manners were not those of the fashionable world, he was caught by their easy playfulness. Of this she was perfectly unaware: to her he was only the man who made himself agreeable nowhere, and who had not thought her handsome enough to dance with.

He began to wish to know more of her; and, as a step towards conversing with her himself, attended to her conversation with others. His doing so drew her notice. It was at Sir William Lucas's, where a large party were assembled.

'What does Mr. Darcy mean?' said she to Charlotte, 'by listening to my conversation with Colonel Forster?'

'That is a question which Mr. Darcy only can answer.'

'But if he does it any more, I shall certainly let him know that I see what he is about. He has a very satirical eye, and if I do not begin by being impertinent myself, I shall soon grow afraid of him.'

On his approaching them soon afterwards, though without seeming to have any intention of speaking, Miss Lucas defied her friend to mention such a subject to him, which immediately provoking Elizabeth to do it, she turned to him and said,—

'Did you not think, Mr. Darcy, that I expressed myself uncommonly well just now, when I was teasing Colonel Forster to give us a ball at Meryton?'

'With great energy; but it is a subject which always makes a lady energetic.'

'You are severe on us.'

'It will be *her* turn soon to be teased,' said Miss Lucas. 'I am going to open the instrument, Eliza, and you know what follows.'

'You are a very strange creature by way of a friend—always wanting me to play and sing before anybody and everybody! If my vanity had taken a musical turn, you would have been invaluable; but as it is, I would really rather not sit down before those who must be in the habit of hearing the very best performers.' On Miss Lucas's persevering, however, she added, 'Very well; if it must be so, it must.' And gravely glancing at Mr. Darcy, 'There is a very fine old saying, which everybody here is of course familiar with—"Keep your breath to cool your porridge,"—and I shall keep mine to swell my song.'

Her performance was pleasing, though by no means capital. After a song or two, and before she could reply to the entreaties of several that she would sing again, she was eagerly succeeded at the instrument by her sister Mary, who having, in consequence of being the only plain one in the family, worked hard for knowledge and accomplishments, was always impatient for display.

Mary had neither genius nor taste; and though vanity had given her application, it had given her likewise a pedantic air and conceited manner, which would have injured a higher degree of excellence than she had reached. Elizabeth, easy and unaffected, had been listened to with much more pleasure, though not playing half so well; and Mary, at the end of a long concerto, was glad to purchase praise and gratitude by Scotch and Irish airs, at the request of her two younger sisters, who with some of the Lucases, and two or three officers, joined eagerly in dancing at one end of the room.

Mr. Darcy stood near them in silent indignation at such a mode of passing the evening, to the exclusion of all conversation, and was much too engrossed by his own thoughts to perceive that Sir William Lucas was his neighbour, till Sir William thus began :—

'What a charming amusement for young people this is, Mr. Darcy! There is nothing like dancing, after all. I consider it as one of the first refinements of polished societies.'

'Certainly, sir; and it has the advantage of being in vogue amongst the less polished societies of the world; every savage can dance.'

Sir William only smiled. 'Your friend performs delightfully,' he continued, after a pause, on seeing Bingley join the group, 'and I doubt not you are an adept in the science yourself, Mr. Darcy.'

'You saw me dance at Meryton, I believe, sir.'

'Yes, indeed, and received no inconsiderable pleasure from the sight. Do you often dance at St. James's?'

'Never, sir.'

'Do you not think it would be a proper compliment to the place?'

'It is a compliment I never pay to any place if I can avoid it.'

'You have a house in town, I conclude.'

Mr. Darcy bowed.

'I had once some thoughts of fixing in town myself, for I am fond of superior society; but I did not feel quite certain that the air in London would agree with Lady Lucas.'

He paused in hopes of an answer; but his companion was not disposed to make any; and Elizabeth at that moment moving towards them, he was struck with the notion of doing a very gallant thing, and called out to her,—

'My dear Miss Eliza, why are you not dancing? Mr. Darcy, you must allow me to present this young lady to you as a very desirable partner. You cannot refuse to dance, I am sure, when so much beauty is before you.' And, taking her hand, he would have given it to Mr. Darcy, who, though extremely surprised, was not unwilling to receive it, when she instantly drew back, and said with some discomposure to Sir William,—

'Indeed, sir, I have not the least intention of

dancing. I entreat you not to suppose that I moved this way in order to beg for a partner.'

Mr. Darcy, with grave propriety, requested to be allowed the honour of her hand, but in vain. Elizabeth was determined; nor did Sir William at all shake her purpose by his attempt at persuasion.

'You excel so much in the dance, Miss Eliza, that it is cruel to deny me the happiness of seeing you; and though this gentleman dislikes the amusement in general, he can have no objection, I am sure, to oblige us for one half-hour.'

'Mr. Darcy is all politeness,' said Elizabeth, smiling.

'He is, indeed: but considering the inducement, my dear Miss Eliza, we cannot wonder at his complaisance: for who would object to such a partner?'

Elizabeth looked archly, and turned away. Her resistance had not injured her with the gentleman, and he was thinking of her with some complacency, when thus accosted by Miss Bingley,—

'I can guess the subject of your reverie.'

'I should imagine not.'

'You are considering how insupportable it would be to pass many evenings in this manner,—in such society; and, indeed, I am quite of your opinion. I was never more annoyed! The insipidity, and yet the noise—the nothingness, and yet the self-importance, of all these people! What would I give to hear your strictures on them!'

'Your conjecture is totally wrong, I assure you. My mind was more agreeably engaged. I have been meditating on the very great pleasure which a pair of fine eyes in the face of a pretty woman can bestow.'

JANE AUSTEN.

Pride and Prejudice.

Miss Sharp's father was an artist, and in that quality had given lessons of drawing at Miss Pinkerton's school. He was a clever man; a pleasant companion; a careless student; with a great propensity for running into debt, and a partiality for the tavern. When he was drunk he used to beat his wife and daughter; and the next morning, with a headache, he would rail at the world for its neglect of his genius, and abuse, with a good deal of cleverness, and sometimes with perfect reason, the fools, his brother painters. As it was with the utmost difficulty that he could keep himself, and as he owed money for a mile round Soho, where he lived, he thought to better his circumstances by marrying a young woman of the French nation, who was by profession an opera-girl. The humble calling of her female parent, Miss Sharp never alluded to, but used to state subsequently that the Entrechats were a noble family of Gascony, and took great pride in her descent from them. And curious it is, that as she advanced in life this young lady's ancestors increased in rank and splendour.

Rebecca's mother had had some education somewhere, and her daughter spoke French with purity and a Parisian accent. It was in those days rather a rare accomplishment, and led to her engagement with the orthodox Miss Pinkerton. For her mother being dead, her father, finding himself not likely to recover, after his third attack of *delirium tremens*, wrote a manly and pathetic letter to Miss Pinkerton, recommending the orphan child to her protection, and so descended to the grave, after two bailiffs had quarrelled over his corpse. Rebecca was seventeen when she came to Chiswick, and was bound over as an articled pupil; her duties being to talk French, as we have seen; and her privileges to live cost free, and, with a few guineas a year, to gather scraps of knowledge from the professors who attended the school.

She was small and slight in person; pale, sandy-haired, with eyes habitually cast down: when they looked up they were very large, odd, and attractive; so attractive, that the Reverend Mr. Crisp, fresh from Oxford, and curate to the Vicar of Chiswick, the Reverend Mr. Flowerdew, fell in love with Miss Sharp; being shot dead by a glance of her eyes which was fired all the way across Chiswick Church from the school-pew to the reading-desk. This infatuated young man used sometimes to take tea with Miss Pinkerton, to whom he had been presented by his mamma, and actually proposed something like marriage in an inter-cepted note, which the one-eyed apple-woman was charged to deliver. Mrs. Crisp was summoned from Buxton, and abruptly carried off her darling boy; but the idea, even, of such an eagle in the Chiswick dovecot caused a great flutter in the breast of Miss

Pinkerton, who would have sent away Miss Sharp but that she was bound to her under a forfeit, and who never could thoroughly believe the young lady's protestations, that she had never exchanged a single word with Mr. Crisp, except under her own eyes on the two occasions when she had met him at tea.

By the side of many tall and bouncing young ladies in the establishment, Rebecca Sharp looked like a child. But she had the dismal precocity of poverty. Many a dun had she talked to, and turned away from her father's door; many a tradesman had she coaxed and wheedled into good-humour, and into the granting of one meal more. She sate commonly with her father, who was very proud of her wit, and heard the talk of many of his wild companions—often but ill-suited for a girl to hear. But she never had been a girl, she said; she had been a woman since she was eight years old. O why did Miss Pinkerton let such a dangerous bird into her cage?

The fact is, the old lady believed Rebecca to be the meekest creature in the world, so admirably, on the occasions when her father brought her to Chiswick, used Rebecca to perform the part of the *ingénue*; and only a year before the arrangement by which Rebecca had been admitted into her house, and when Rebecca was sixteen years old, Miss Pinkerton majestically, and with a little speech, made her a present of a doll — which was, by the way, the confiscated property of Miss Swindle, discovered surreptitiously nursing it in school-hours. How the father and daughter laughed as they trudged home together after the evening party (it was on the occasion of the speeches, when all the professors were invited), and how Miss Pinkerton would have raged had she seen the caricature of herself which the little mimic, Rebecca, managed to make out of her doll. Becky used to go through dialogues with it; it formed the delight of Newman Street, Gerrard Street, and the Artists' quarter: and the young painters, when they came to take their gin-and-water with their lazy, dissolute, clever, jovial senior, used regularly to ask Rebecca if Miss Pinkerton was at home: she was as well known to them, poor soul! as Mr. Lawrence or President West. Once Rebecca had the honour to pass a few days at Chiswick; after which she brought back Jemima, and erected another doll as Miss Jemmy: for though that honest creature had made and given her jelly and cake enough for three children, and a seven-shilling piece at parting, the girl's sense of ridicule was far stronger than her gratitude, and she sacrificed Miss Jemmy quite as pitilessly as her sister.

The catastrophe came, and she was brought to the Mall as to her home. The rigid formality of the place suffocated her: the prayers and the meals, the lessons and the walks, which were arranged with a conventual regularity, oppressed her almost beyond endurance; and she looked back to the freedom and the beggary of the old studio in Soho with so much regret, that everybody, herself included, fancied she

MAUD IS ONLY SEVENTEEN

Page 194

" Maud is only seventeen,
But she is tall and stately.

TENNYSON   "Maud."

was consumed with grief for her father. She had a little room in the garret, where the maids heard her walking and sobbing at night; but it was with rage, and not with grief. She had not been much of a dissembler, until now her loneliness taught her to feign. She had never mingled in the society of women : her father, reprobate as he was, was a man of talent; his conversation was a thousand times more agreeable to her than the talk of such of her own sex as she now encountered. The pompous vanity of the old schoolmistress, the foolish good-humour of her sister, the silly chat and scandal of the elder girls, and the frigid correctness of the governesses equally annoyed her; and she had no soft maternal heart, this unlucky girl, otherwise the prattle and talk of the younger children, with whose care she was chiefly entrusted, might have soothed and interested her; but she lived among them two years, and not one was sorry that she went away. The gentle tender-hearted Amelia Sedley was the only person to whom she could attach herself in the least; and who could help attaching herself to Amelia ?

The happiness—the superior advantages of the young women around her, gave Rebecca inexpressible pangs of envy. 'What airs that girl gives herself because she is an Earl's grand-daughter,' she said of one. 'How they cringe and bow to that Creole, because of her hundred thousand pounds! I am a thousand times cleverer and more charming than that creature, for all her wealth. I am as well-bred as the

N

Earl's grand-daughter, for all her fine pedigree; and yet every one passes me by here.   And yet, when I was at my father's, did not the men give up their gayest balls and parties in order to pass the evening with me?'   She determined at any rate to get free from the prison in which she found herself, and now began to act for herself, and for the first time to make connected plans for the future.

W. M. THACKERAY.

Vanity Fair.

TO FANNY

I CRY your mercy—pity—love!—aye, love!
　　Merciful love that tantalises not,
One-thoughted, never-wandering, guileless love,
　　Unmask'd, and being seen—without a blot!
O! let me have thee whole,—all—all—be mine!
　　That shape, that fairness, that sweet minor zest
Of love, your kiss—those hands, those eyes divine,
　　That warm, white, lucent, million - pleasured
　　　　breast,—
Yourself—your soul—in pity give me all,
　　Withhold no atom's atom or I die,
Or living on perhaps, your wretched thrall,
　　Forget, in the mist of idle misery,
Life's purposes,—the palate of my mind
Losing its gust, and my ambition blind!

JOHN KEATS.

MRS. SIDDONS

As when a child on some long winter's night,
Affrighted clinging to its grandam's knees,
With eager wond'ring and perturb'd delight
Listens strange tales of fearful dark decrees
Mutter'd to wretch by necromantic spell;
Or of those hags, who at the witching time
Of murky midnight ride the air sublime,
And mingle foul embrace with fiends of hell:
Cold horror drinks its blood! Anon the tear
More gentle starts, to hear the beldame tell
Of pretty babes, that loved each other dear,
Murder'd by cruel uncle's mandate fell:
Ev'n so the shiv'ring joys thy tones impart,
Ev'n so thou, Siddons! meltest my sad heart!

SAMUEL TAYLOR COLERIDGE.

THE SOLITARY REAPER

BEHOLD her, single in the field,
Yon solitary Highland lass!
Reaping and singing by herself;
Stop here, or gently pass!
Alone she cuts and binds the grain,
And sings a melancholy strain;
O listen! for the vale profound
Is overflowing with the sound.

No nightingale did ever chaunt
More welcome notes to weary bands
Of travellers in some shady haunt,
Among Arabian sands:
A voice so thrilling ne'er was heard
In spring-time from the cuckoo-bird,
Breaking the silence of the seas
Among the farthest Hebrides.

Will no one tell me what she sings?
Perhaps the plaintive numbers flow
For old, unhappy, far-off things,
And battles long ago:
Or is it some more humble lay,
Familiar matters of to-day?
Some natural sorrow, loss, or pain,
That has been, and may be again!

N 2

Whate'er the theme, the Maiden sang
As if her song could have no ending;
I saw her singing at her work,
And o'er the sickle bending;—
I listened, motionless and still;
And, as I mounted up the hill,
The music in my heart I bore,
Long after it was heard no more.

WILLIAM WORDSWORTH.

FAIR INES

O saw ye not fair Ines?
    She's gone into the West,
To dazzle when the sun is down,
    And rob the world of rest:
She took our daylight with her,
    The smiles that we love best,
With morning blushes on her cheek,
    And pearls upon her breast.

O turn again, fair Ines,
    Before the fall of night,
For fear the moon should shine alone,
    And stars unrivalled bright;
And blessèd will the lover be
    That walks beneath their light,
And breathes the love against thy cheek
    I dare not even write!

Would I had been, fair Ines,
    That gallant cavalier
Who rode so gaily by thy side,
    And whispered thee so near!
Were there no bonny dames at home,
    Or no true lovers here,
That he should cross the seas to win
    The dearest of the dear?

I saw thee, lovely Ines,
　　Descend along the shore,
With bands of noble gentlemen,
　　And banners waved before,
And gentle youths and maidens gay—
　　And snowy plumes they wore :
It would have been a beauteous dream—
　　If it had been no more !

Alas, alas, fair Ines !
　　She went away with song,
With music waiting on her steps,
　　And shoutings of the throng :
But some were sad and felt no mirth,
　　But only music's wrong,
In sounds that sang, Farewell, farewell,
　　To her you 've loved so long.

Farewell, farewell, fair Ines !
　　That vessel never bore
So fair a lady on its deck,
　　Nor danced so light before.
Alas, for pleasure on the sea,
　　And sorrow on the shore !
The smile that blest one lover's heart
　　Has broken many more !

THOMAS HOOD.

MRS. GAMP

Mrs. Gamp had a large bundle with her, a pair of pattens, and a species of gig umbrella; the latter article in colour like a faded leaf, except where a circular patch of livery blue had been dexterously let in at the top. She was much flurried by the haste she had made, and laboured under the most erroneous views of cabriolets, which she appeared to confound with mail-coaches or stage-waggons, inasmuch as she was constantly endeavouring for the first half mile to force her luggage through the little front window, and clamouring to the driver to 'put it in the boot.' When she was disabused of this idea, her whole being resolved itself into an absorbing anxiety about her pattens, with which she played innumerable games of quoits, on Mr. Pecksniff's legs. It was not until they were close upon the house of mourning that she had enough composure to observe:

'And so the gentleman's dead, sir! Ah! The more's the pity'—she didn't even know his name. 'But it's what we must all come to. It's as certain as being born, except that we can't make our calculations as exact. Ah! Poor dear!'

She was a fat old woman, this Mrs. Gamp, with a husky voice and a moist eye, which she had a remarkable power of turning up, and only showing the white of. Having very little neck, it cost her some trouble to look over herself, if one may say so, at those to whom she talked. She wore a very rusty black gown, rather the worse for snuff, and a shawl and bonnet to correspond. In these dilapidated articles of dress she had, on principle, arrayed herself, time out of mind, on such occasions as the present; for this at once expressed a decent amount of veneration for the deceased, and invited the next-of-kin to present her with a fresher suit of weeds: an appeal so frequently successful, that the very fetich and ghost of Mrs. Gamp, bonnet and all, might be seen hanging up, any hour in the day, in at least a dozen of the second-hand clothes shops about Holborn. The face of Mrs. Gamp — the nose in particular — was somewhat red and swollen, and it was difficult to enjoy her society without becoming conscious of a smell of spirits. Like most persons who have attained to great eminence in their profession, she took to hers very kindly; insomuch, that setting aside her natural predilections as a woman, she went to a lying-in or a laying-out with equal zest and relish.

'Ah!' repeated Mrs. Gamp; for it was always a safe sentiment in case of mourning. 'Ah dear! When Gamp was summoned to his long home, and I see him a-lying in Guy's Hospital with a penny-piece on each eye, and his wooden leg under his left arm, I thought I should have fainted away. But I bore up.'

If certain whispers current in Kingsgate Street circles had any truth in them, she had indeed borne up surprisingly; and had exerted such uncommon fortitude, as to dispose of Mr. Gamp's remains for the benefit of science. But it should be added, in fairness, that this had happened twenty years ago; and that Mr. and Mrs. Gamp had long been separated, on the ground of incompatibility of temper in their drink.

'You have become indifferent since then, I suppose?' said Mr. Pecksniff. 'Use is second nature, Mrs. Gamp.'

'You may well say second nater, sir,' returned that lady. 'One's first ways is to find sich things a trial to the feelings; and so is one's lasting custom. If it wasn't for the nerve a little sip of liquor gives me (I never was able to do more than taste it), I never could go through with what I sometimes have to do. "Mrs. Harris," I says, at the very last case as ever I acted in, which it was but a young person; "Mrs. Harris," I sez, "leave the bottle on the chimbley-piece, and don't ask me to take none, but let me put my lips to it when I am so dispoged, and then I will do what I'm engaged to do, according to the best of my ability." "Mrs. Gamp," says she, in answer, "if ever there was a sober creetur to be got at eighteen pence a day for working people, and three and six for gentlefolks— night watching,"' said Mrs. Gamp, with emphasis, '"being a extra charge—you are that inwalable person." "Mrs. Harris," I says to her, "don't name the charge, for if I could afford to lay all my feller creeturs out for nothink, I would gladly do it; sich is the love I bear 'em. But what I always says to them as has the management of matters, Mrs. Harris "'—here she kept her eye on Mr. Pecksniff—'"be they gents or be they ladies—is, don't ask me whether I won't take none, or whether I will, but leave the bottle on the chimbley-piece, and let me put my lips to it when I am so dispoged."'

CHARLES DICKENS.

Martin Chuzzlewit.

KATE BARLASS

" And now the rush was heard on the stair,
And 'God what help!' was our cry,
And was I frenzied or was I bold ?
I looked at each empty stanchion-hold,
And no bar but my arm had I."

D. G. ROSSETTI. "The King's Tragedy."

MRS. CAUDLE

*Mr. Caudle has ventured a remonstrance on his day's
dinner: cold mutton, and no pudding.—Mrs.
Caudle defends the cold shoulder.*

'Umph! I'm sure! Well! I wonder what it will
be next? There's nothing proper, now—nothing at
all. Better get somebody else to keep the house, I
think. I can't do it now, it seems; I'm only in the
way here: I'd better take the children, and go.

'What am I grumbling about now? It's all very
well for you to ask that! I'm sure I'd better be out
of the world than—there now, Mr. Caudle; there you
go again! I *shall* speak, sir. It isn't often I open
my mouth, Heaven knows! But you like to hear
nobody talk but yourself. You ought to have married
a negro slave, and not any respectable woman.

'You're to go about the house looking like thunder
all the day, and I'm not to say a word. Where do
you think pudding's to come from every day? You
show a nice example to your children, you do; com-
plaining, and turning your nose up at a sweet piece
of cold mutton, because there's no pudding! You
go a nice way to make 'em extravagant—teach 'em
nice lessons to begin the world with. Do you know

o

what puddings cost; do you think they fly in at the window?

'You hate cold mutton? The more shame for you, Mr. Caudle. I'm sure you've the stomach of a lord, you have. No, sir: I didn't choose to hash the mutton. It's very easy for you to say hash it; but *I* know what a joint loses in hashing: it's a day's dinner the less, if it's a bit. Yes, I daresay; other people may have puddings with cold mutton. No doubt of it; and other people become bankrupts. But if ever you get into the *Gazette*, it sha'n't be my fault—no; I'll do my duty as a wife to you, Mr. Caudle; you shall never have it to say that it was *my* housekeeping that brought you to beggary. No; you may sulk at the cold meat—ha! I hope you'll never live to want such a piece of cold meat as we had to-day! and you may threaten to go to a tavern to dine; but, with our present means, not a crumb of pudding do you get from me. You shall have nothing but the cold joint—nothing, as I'm a Christian sinner.

'Yes; there you are, throwing those fowls in my face again! I know you once brought home a pair of fowls; I know it: and weren't you mean enough to want to stop 'em out of my week's money? Oh! the selfishness—the shabbiness of men! They can go out and throw away pounds upon pounds with a pack of people who laugh at 'em afterwards; but if it's anything wanted for their own homes, their poor wives may hunt for it. I wonder you don't blush to name those fowls again! I wouldn't be so little for the world, Mr. Caudle.

'What are you going to do?

'*Going to get up?*

'Don't make yourself ridiculous, Mr. Caudle; I can't say a word to you like any other wife, but you must threaten to get up. *Do* be ashamed of yourself.

'Puddings, indeed! Do you think I'm made of puddings? Didn't you have some boiled rice three weeks ago? Besides, is this the time of the year for puddings? It's all very well if I had money enough allowed me like any other wife to keep the house with: then, indeed, I might have preserves like any other woman; now, it's impossible; and it's cruel—yes, Mr. Caudle, cruel—of you to expect it.

'*Apples aren't so dear, are they?*

'I know what apples are, Mr. Caudle, without your telling me. But I suppose you want something more than apples for dumplings? I suppose sugar costs something, doesn't it? And that's how it is. That's how one expense brings on another, and that's how people go to ruin.

'*Pancakes?*

'What's the use of your lying muttering there about pancakes? Don't you always have 'em once a year—every Shrove Tuesday? And what would any moderate decent man want more?

'Pancakes, indeed! Pray, Mr. Caudle—no, it's no use your saying fine words to me to let you go to sleep : I sha'n't—pray do you know the price of eggs just now ? There 's not an egg you can trust to under seven and eight a shilling ; well, you 've only just to reckon up how many eggs—don't lie swearing there at the eggs in that manner, Mr. Caudle ; unless you expect the bed to let you fall through. You call yourself a respectable tradesman, I suppose ? Ha ! I only wish people knew you as well as I do ! Swearing at eggs, indeed ! But I 'm tired of this usage, Mr. Caudle ; quite tired of it ; and I don't care how soon it 's ended !

'I 'm sure I do nothing but work and labour, and think how to make the most of everything ; and this is how I 'm rewarded. I should like to see anybody whose joints go further than mine. But if I was to throw away your money into the street, or lay it out in fine feathers on myself, I should be better thought of. The woman who studies her husband and her family is always made a drudge of. It 's your fine fal-lal wives who 've the best time of it.

'What 's the use of your lying groaning there in that manner ? That won't make me hold my tongue, I can tell you. You think to have it all your own way —but you won't, Mr. Caudle ! You can insult my dinner ; look like a demon, I may say, at a wholesome piece of cold mutton—ah ! the thousands of far better creatures than you are who 'd be thankful for that mutton !—and I 'm never to speak ! But you 're mistaken—I will. Your usage of me, Mr. Caudle, is infamous—unworthy of a man. I only wish people knew you for what you are; but I've told you again and again they shall some day.

'Puddings? And now I suppose I shall hear of nothing but puddings! Yes, and I know what it would end in. First, you'd have a pudding every day — oh, I know your extravagance — then you'd go for fish—then, I shouldn't wonder if you'd have soup; turtle, no doubt: then you'd go for dessert; and—oh! I see it all as plain as the quilt before me —but no, not while I'm alive! What your second wife may do, I don't know; perhaps *she'll* be a fine lady; but you sha'n't be ruined by me, Mr. Caudle; that I'm determined. Puddings, indeed! pu-dding-s! Pud——'

'*Exhausted nature*,' says Mr. Caudle, '*could hold out no longer. She went to sleep.*'

DOUGLAS JERROLD.
Mrs. Caudle's Curtain Lectures.

o 2

TO HELEN

Helen, thy beauty is to me
  Like those Nicéan barks of yore
That gently, o'er a perfumed sea,
  The weary way-worn wanderer bore
  To his own native shore.

On desperate seas long wont to roam,
  Thy hyacinth hair, thy classic face,
Thy Naiad airs have brought me home
  To the glory that was Greece,
  And the grandeur that was Rome.

Lo, in yon brilliant window-niche
  How statue-like I see. thee stand,
  The agate lamp within thy hand!
Ah, Psyche, from the regions which
  Are holy land!

EDGAR ALLAN POE.

JENNY KISSED ME

Jenny kiss'd me when we met,
    Jumping from the chair she sat in;
Time, you thief, who love to get
    Sweets into your list, put that in:
Say I'm weary, say I'm sad,
    Say that health and wealth have miss'd me,
Say I'm growing old, but add,
    Jenny kiss'd me.

LEIGH HUNT.

MAUD MULLER

Maud Muller, on a summer's day,
Raked the meadow sweet with hay.

Beneath her torn hat glowed the wealth
Of simple beauty and rustic health.

Singing, she wrought, and her merry glee
The mock-bird echoed from his tree.

But when she glanced to the far-off town,
White from its hill-slope looking down,

The sweet song died, and a vague unrest
And a nameless longing filled her breast,—

A wish, that she hardly dared to own,
For something better than she had known.

The Judge rode slowly down the lane,
Smoothing his horse's chestnut mane.

He drew his bridle in the shade
Of the apple-trees, to greet the maid,

And ask a draught from the spring that flowed
Through the meadow across the road.

She stooped where the cool spring bubbled up,
And filled for him her small tin cup,

And blushed as she gave it, looking down
On her feet so bare, and her tattered gown.

'Thanks,' said the Judge; 'a sweeter draught
From a fairer hand was never quaffed.'

He spoke of the grass and flowers and trees,
Of the singing birds and the humming bees;

Then talked of the haying, and wondered whether
The cloud in the west would bring foul weather.

And Maud forgot her brier-torn gown,
And her graceful ankles bare and brown;

And listened, while a pleased surprise
Looked from her long-lashed hazel eyes.

At last, like one who for delay
Seeks a vain excuse, he rode away.

Maud Muller looked and sighed: 'Ah me!
That I the Judge's bride might be!

'He would dress me up in silks so fine,
And praise and toast me at his wine.

'My father should wear a broadcloth coat ;
My brother should sail a painted boat.

'I 'd dress my mother so grand and gay,
And the baby should have a new toy each day.

'And I 'd feed the hungry and clothe the poor,
And all should bless me who left our door.'

And the Judge looked back as he climbed the hill,
And saw Maud Muller standing still.

'A form more fair, a face more sweet,
Ne'er hath it been my lot to meet.

'And her modest answer and graceful air
Show her wise and good as she is fair.

'Would she were mine, and I to-day,
Like her, a harvester of hay

'No doubtful balance of rights and wrongs,
Nor weary lawyers with endless tongues,

'But low of cattle and song of birds,
And health and quiet and loving words.'

But he thought of his sisters proud and cold,
And his mother vain of her rank and gold.

So, closing his heart, the Judge rode on,
And Maud was left in the field alone.

But the lawyers smiled that afternoon,
When he hummed in court an old love-tune;

And the young girl mused beside the well,
Till the rain on the unraked clover fell.

He wedded a wife of richest dower,
Who lived for fashion, as he for power.

Yet oft in his marble hearth's bright glow,
He watched a picture come and go;

And sweet Maud Muller's hazel eyes
Looked out in their innocent surprise.

Oft, when the wine in his glass was red,
He longed for the wayside well instead;

And closed his eyes on his garnished rooms,
To dream of meadows, and clover-blooms.

And the proud man sighed, with a secret pain,
'Ah, that I were free again!

'Free as when I rode that day,
Where the barefoot maiden raked her hay.'

She wedded a man unlearned and poor,
And many children played round their door.

But care and sorrow, and childbirth pain,
Left their trace on her heart and brain.

And oft, when the summer sun shone hot
On the new-mown hay in the meadow lot,

And she heard the little spring brook fall
Over the roadside, through the wall,

In the shade of the apple-tree again,
She saw a rider draw his rein,

And, gazing down with timid grace,
She felt his pleased eyes read her face.

Sometimes her narrow kitchen walls
Stretched away into shady halls;

The weary wheel to a spinet turned,
The tallow candle an astral burned,

And for him who sat by the chimney lug,
Dozing and grumbling o'er pipe and mug,

A manly form at her side she saw,
And joy was duty and love was law.

ST. CATHERINE

St. Catherine of Siena, negociating with Pope Gregory XI. on behalf of the Florentines.

Then she took up her burden of life again,
Saying only, 'It might have been.'

Alas for Maiden, alas for Judge,
For rich repiner and household drudge!

God pity them both! and pity us all!
Who vainly the dreams of youth recall.

For of all sad words of tongue or pen,
The saddest are these: 'It might have been!'

Ah, well! for us all some sweet hope lies
Deeply buried from human eyes;

And, in the hereafter, angels may
Roll the stone from its grave away.

JOHN GREENLEAF WHITTIER.

'MISS MOWCHER!'

I looked at the doorway and saw nothing. I was still looking at the doorway, thinking that Miss Mowcher was a long while making her appearance, when, to my infinite astonishment, there came waddling round the sofa which stood between me and it, a pursy dwarf, of about forty or forty-five, with a very large head and face, a pair of roguish grey eyes, and such extremely little arms, that, to enable herself to lay a finger archly against her snub nose as she ogled Steerforth, she was obliged to meet the finger half-way, and lay her nose against it. Her chin, which was what is called a double chin, was so fat that it entirely swallowed up the strings of her bonnet, bow and all. Throat she had none; waist she had none; legs she had none worth mentioning; for though she was more than full-sized down to where her waist would have been, if she had had any, and though she terminated, as human beings generally do, in a pair of feet, she was so short that she stood at a common-sized chair as at a table, resting a bag she carried on the seat. This lady; dressed in an off-hand, easy style; bringing her nose and her fore-finger together, with the difficulty I have described; standing with her head necessarily on one side, and, with one of her sharp eyes shut up, making an uncommonly knowing face; after ogling Steerforth for a few moments, broke into a torrent of words.

'What! My flower!' she pleasantly began, shaking her large head at him. 'You're there, are you! Oh, you naughty boy, fie for shame, what do you do so far away from home? Up to mischief, I'll be bound. Oh, you're a downy fellow, Steerforth, so you are, and I'm another, ain't I? Ha, ha, ha! You'd have betted a hundred pounds to five, now, that you wouldn't have seen me here, wouldn't you? Bless you, man alive, I'm everywhere. I'm here, and there, and where not, like the conjuror's half-crown in the lady's hand-kercher. Talking of handkerchers—*and* talking of ladies — what a comfort you are to your blessed mother, ain't you, my dear boy, over one of my shoulders, and I don't say which!'

Miss Mowcher untied her bonnet, at this passage of her discourse, threw back the strings, and sat down, panting, on a foot-stool in front of the fire—making a kind of arbour of the dining-table, which spread its mahogany shelter above her head.

'Oh my stars and what's-their-name!' she went on, clapping a hand on each of her little knees, and glancing shrewdly at me. 'I'm of too full a habit, that's the fact, Steerforth. After a flight of stairs, it gives me as much trouble to draw every breath I want, as if it was a bucket of water. If you saw me looking out of an upper window, you'd think I was a fine woman, wouldn't you?'

'I should think that, wherever I saw you,' replied Steerforth.

'Go along, you dog, do!' cried the little creature, making a whisk at him with the handkerchief with which she was wiping her face, 'and don't be impudent! But I give you my word and honour I was at Lady Mithers' last week—*there's* a woman! How *she* wears! —And Mithers himself came into the room where I was waiting for her—*there's* a man! How *he* wears! and his wig too, for he's had it these ten years—and he went on at that rate in the complimentary line, that I began to think I should be obliged to ring the bell. Ha! ha! ha! He's a pleasant wretch, but he wants principle.'

'What were you doing for Lady Mithers?' asked Steerforth.

'That's tellings, my blessed infant,' she retorted, tapping her nose again, screwing up her face, and twinkling her eyes like an imp of supernatural intelligence. 'Never *you* mind! You'd like to know whether I stop her hair from falling off, or dye it, or touch up her complexion, or improve her eyebrows, wouldn't you? Do you know what my great-grandfather's name was?'

'No,' said Steerforth.

'It was Walker, my sweet pet,' replied Miss Mowcher, 'and he came of a long line of Walkers, that I inherit all the Hookey èstate from.'

I never beheld anything approaching to Miss Mowcher's wink, except Miss Mowcher's self-possession. She had a wonderful way too, when listening to what was said to her, or when waiting for an answer to what she had said herself, of pausing with her head cunningly on one side, and one eye turned up like a magpie's. Altogether I was lost in amazement, and sat staring at her, quite oblivious, I am afraid, of the laws of politeness.

She had by this time drawn the chair to her side, and was busily engaged in producing from her bag (plunging in her short arm to the shoulder, at every dive) a number of small bottles, sponges, combs, brushes, bits of flannel, little pairs of curling-irons, and other instruments, which she tumbled in a heap upon the chair. From this employment she suddenly desisted, and said to Steerforth, much to my confusion.

'Who's your friend?'

'Mr. Copperfield,' said Steerforth; 'he wants to know you.'

'Well, then, he shall! I thought he looked as if he did!' returned Miss Mowcher, waddling up to me, bag in hand, and laughing on me as she came. 'Face like a peach!' standing on tiptoe to pinch my cheek as I sat. 'Quite tempting! I'm very fond of peaches. Happy to make your acquaintances, Mr. Copperfield, I'm sure.'

I said I congratulated myself on having the honour to make hers, and that the happiness was mutual.

'Oh my goodness, how polite we are!' exclaimed Miss Mowcher, making a preposterous attempt to

p 2

cover her large face with her morsel of a hand. 'What a world of gammon and spinnage it is, though, ain't it?'

This was addressed confidentially to both of us, as the morsel of a hand came away from the face, and buried itself, arm and all, in the bag again.

'What do you mean, Miss Mowcher?' said Steerforth.

'Ha! ha! ha! What a refreshing set of humbugs we are, to be sure, ain't we, my sweet child?' replied that morsel of a woman, feeling in the bag with her head on one side, and her eye in the air. 'Look here!' taking something out. 'Scraps of the Russian Prince's nails! Prince Alphabet turned topsy-turvy, *I* call him, for his name's got all the letters in it, higgledy-piggledy.'

'The Russian Prince is a client of yours, is he?' said Steerforth.

'I believe you, my pet,' replied Miss Mowcher. 'I keep his nails in order for him. Twice a week! Fingers *and* toes!'

'He pays well, I hope,' said Steerforth.

'Pays as he speaks, my dear child,—through the nose,' replied Miss Mowcher. 'None of your close shavers the Prince ain't. You'd say so, if you saw his moustachios. Red by nature, black by art.'

'By your art, of course,' said Steerforth.

Miss Mowcher winked assent. 'Forced to send for me. Couldn't help it. The climate affected *his* dye; it did very well in Russia, but it was no go here!

You never saw such a rusty prince in all your born days as he was. Like old iron!'

'Is that why you called him a humbug, just now?' inquired Steerforth.

'Oh, you're a broth of a boy, ain't you?' returned Miss Mowcher, shaking her head violently. 'I said, what a set of humbugs we were in general, and I showed you the scraps of the Prince's nails to prove it. The Prince's nails do more for me in private families of the genteel sort, than all my talents put together. I always carry 'em about. They're the best introduction. If Miss Mowcher cuts the Prince's nails, she *must* be all right. I give 'em away to the young ladies. They put 'em in albums, I believe. Ha! ha! ha! Upon my life, "the whole social system" (as the men call it when they make speeches in Parliament) is a system of Prince's nails!' said this least of women, trying to fold her short arms, and nodding her large head.

Steerforth laughed heartily, and I laughed too, Miss Mowcher continuing all the time to shake her head (which was very much on one side), and look into the air with one eye, and to wink with the other.

'Well, well!' she said, smiting her small knees, and rising, 'this is not business. Come, Steerforth, let's explore the polar regions, and have it over.'

She then selected two or three of the little instruments and a little bottle, and asked (to my surprise) if the table would bear. On Steerforth's replying in the affirmative, she pushed a chair against it, and begging the assistance of my hand, mounted up, pretty nimbly, to the top, as if it were a stage.

'If either of you saw my ankles,' she said, when she was safely elevated, 'say so, and I'll go home and destroy myself.' .

'*I* did not,' said Steerforth.

'*I* did not,' said I.

'Well then,' cried Miss Mowcher, 'I'll consent to live. Now, ducky, ducky, ducky, come to Mrs. Bond and be killed.'

This was an invocation to Steerforth to place himself under her hands; who, accordingly, sat himself down, with his back to the table, and his laughing face towards me, and submitted his head to her inspection, evidently for no other purpose than our entertainment. To see Miss Mowcher standing over him, looking at his rich profusion of brown hair through a large round magnifying-glass, which she took out of her pocket, was a most amazing spectacle.

'*You're* a pretty fellow!' said Miss Mowcher, after a brief inspection. 'You'd be as bald as a friar on the top of your head in twelve months, but for me. Just half-a-minute, my young friend, and we'll give you a polishing that shall keep your curls on for the next ten years!'

CHARLES DICKENS.
David Copperfield.

TO IANTHE

You smil'd, you spoke, and I believed,
By every smile and word deceived.
Another man would hope no more;
Nor hope I what I hoped before:
But let not this last wish be vain;
Deceive—deceive me once again!

WALTER SAVAGE LANDOR.

ROSE AYLMER

Ah, what avails the sceptred race,
    Ah, what the form divine!
What every virtue, every grace!
    Rose Aylmer, all were thine.

Rose Aylmer, whom these wakeful eyes
    May weep, but never see,
A night of memories and of sighs
    I consecrate to thee.

WALTER SAVAGE LANDOR.

THE boy knocked at the door, and the door promptly opened with a spring and a click. A parlour door within a small entry stood open, and disclosed a child —a dwarf—a girl—a something—sitting on a little low old-fashioned arm-chair, which had a kind of little working bench before it.

'I can't get up,' said the child, 'because my back's bad, and my legs are queer. But I'm the person of the house.'

'Who else is at home?' asked Charley Hexam, staring.

'Nobody's at home at present,' returned the child, with a glib assertion of her dignity, 'except the person of the house. What did you want, young man?'

'I wanted to see my sister.'

'Many young men have sisters,' returned the child. 'Give me your name, young man.'

The queer little figure, and the queer but not ugly little face with its bright grey eyes, were so sharp, that the sharpness of the manner seemed unavoidable. As if, being turned out of that mould, it must be sharp.

'Hexam is my name.'

'Ah, indeed?' said the person of the house. 'I

thought it might be. Your sister will be in in about a quarter of an hour. I am very fond of your sister. She's my particular friend. Take a seat. And this gentleman's name?'

'Mr. Headstone, my schoolmaster.'

'Take a seat. And would you please to shut the street door first? I can't very well do it myself, because my back's so bad, and my legs are so queer.'

They complied in silence, and the little figure went on with its work of gumming and gluing together with a camel's-hair brush certain pieces of cardboard and thin wool previously cut into various shapes. The scissors and knives upon the bench showed that the child herself had cut them; and the bright scraps of velvet and silk and ribbon also strewn upon the bench showed that when duly stuffed (and stuffing too was there), she was to cover them smartly. The dexterity of her nimble fingers was remarkable, and, as she brought two thin edges accurately together by giving them a little bite, she would glance at the visitors out of the corners of her grey eyes with a look that out-sharpened all her other sharpness.

'You can't tell me the name of my trade, I'll be bound,' she said, after taking several of these observations.

'You make pin-cushions,' said Charley.

'What else do I make?'

'Pen-wipers,' said Bradley Headstone.

'Ha! ha! What else do I make? You're a schoolmaster, but you can't tell me.'

'You do something,' he returned, pointing to a corner of the little bench, 'with straw, but I don't know what.'

'Well done you!' cried the person of the house. 'I only make pin-cushions and pen-wipers to use up my waste. But my straw really does belong to my business. Try again. What do I make with my straw?'

'Dinner-mats.'

'A schoolmaster, and says dinner-mats! I'll give you a clue to my trade, in a game of forfeits. I love my love with a B because she's Beautiful; I hate my love with a B because she is brazen; I took her to the sign of the Blue Boar, and I treated her with Bonnets; her name's Bouncer, and she lives in Bedlam.—Now, what do I make with my straw?'

'Ladies' bonnets?'

'Fine ladies',' said the person of the house, nodding assent. 'Dolls'. I'm a Doll's Dressmaker.'

'I hope it's a good business?'

The person of the house shrugged her shoulders and shook her head. 'No. Poorly paid. And I'm often so pressed for time! I had a doll married, last week, and was obliged to work all night. But it's not good for me, on account of my back being so bad and my legs so queer.'

They looked at the little creature with a wonder that did not diminish, and the schoolmaster said: 'I'm sorry your fine ladies are so inconsiderate.'

'It's the way with them,' said the person of the

ST. CLARE

St. Clare in the garden of one of the Monasteries she founded after she had given her fortune to the poor.

house, shrugging her shoulders again. 'And they take no care of their clothes, and they never keep to the same fashions a month. I work for a doll with three daughters. Bless you, she's enough to ruin her husband!'

The person of the house gave a weird little laugh here, and gave them another look out of the corners of her eyes. She had an elfin chin that was capable of great expression; and whenever she gave this look, she hitched this chin up. As if her eyes and chin worked together on the same wires.

'Are you always as busy as you are now?'

'Busier. I'm slack just now. I finished a large mourning order the day before yesterday. Doll I work for lost a canary-bird.' The person of the house gave another little laugh, and then nodded her head several times, as who should moralise, 'Oh this world, this world!'

'Are you alone all day?' asked Bradley Headstone. 'Don't any of the neighbouring children——'

'Ah, lud!' cried the person of the house, with a little scream, as if the word had pricked her. 'Don't talk of children. I can't bear children. _I_ know their tricks and manners.' She said this with an angry little shake of her right fist close before her eyes.

Perhaps it scarcely required the teacher-habit to perceive that the doll's dressmaker was inclined to be bitter on the difference between herself and other children, but both master and pupil understood it so.

Q

'Always running about and screeching, always playing and fighting, always skip-skip-skipping on the pavement and chalking it for their games! Oh! *I* know their tricks and their manners!' shaking the little fist as before. 'And that's not all. Ever so often calling names in through a person's keyhole, and imitating a person's back and legs. Oh! *I* know their tricks and their manners. And I'll tell you what I'd do to punish 'em. There's doors under the church in the square—black doors, leading into black vaults. Well! I'd open one of those doors, and I'd cram 'em all in, and then I'd lock the door, and through the keyhole I'd blow in pepper.'

'What would be the good of blowing in pepper?' asked Charley Hexam.

'To set 'em sneezing,' said the person of the house, 'and make their eyes water. And when they were all sneezing and inflamed, I'd mock 'em through the keyhole, just as they, with their tricks and manners, mock a person through a person's keyhole!'

An uncommonly emphatic shake of her little fist close before her eyes seemed to ease the mind of the person of the house; for she added with recovered composure, 'No, no, no. No children for me. Give me grown-ups.'

It was difficult to guess the age of this strange creature, for her poor figure furnished no clue to it, and her face was at once so young and so old. Twelve, or at the most thirteen, might be near the mark.

'I always did like grown-ups,' she went on, 'and

always kept company with them. So sensible. Sit so quiet. Don't go prancing and capering about! And I mean always to keep among none but grown-ups till I marry. I suppose I must make up my mind to marry, one of these days.'

She listened to a step outside that caught her ear, and there was a soft knock at the door. Pulling at a handle within her reach, she said with a pleased laugh: 'Now here, for instance, is a grown-up that's my particular friend!' and Lizzie Hexam in a black dress entered the room.

CHARLES DICKENS.
Our Mutual Friend.

MAUD

BIRDS in the high Hall-garden
    When twilight was falling,
Maud, Maud, Maud, Maud,
    They were crying and calling.

Where was Maud? in our wood;
    And I, who else, was with her,
Gathering woodland lilies,
    Myriads blow together.

Birds in our wood sang
    Ringing thro' the valleys,
Maud is here, here, here
    In among the lilies.

I kiss'd her slender hand,
    She took the kiss sedately;
Maud is not seventeen,
    But she is tall and stately.

I to cry out on pride
    Who have won her favour!
O Maud were sure of Heaven
    If lowliness could save her.

I know the way she went
    Home with her maiden posy,
For her feet have touch'd the meadows
    And left the daisies rosy.

                                    TENNYSON.

THE lady, whom I had never seen before, lifted up her eyes and looked archly at me, and then I saw that the eyes were Estella's eyes. But she was so much changed, was so much more beautiful, so much more womanly, in all things winning admiration had made such wonderful advance, that I seemed to have made none. I fancied, as I looked at her, that I slipped hopelessly back into the coarse and common boy again. O, the sense of distance and disparity that came upon me, and the inaccessibility that came about her!

She gave me her hand. I stammered something about the pleasure I felt in seeing her again, and about my having looked forward to it for a long, long time.

'Do you find her much changed, Pip?' asked Miss Havisham, with her greedy look, and striking her stick upon a chair that stood between them, as a sign to me to sit down there.

'When I came in, Miss Havisham, I thought there was nothing of Estella in the face or figure; but now it all settles down so curiously into the old——'

'What? You are not going to say into the old Estella?' Miss Havisham interrupted. 'She was

Q 2

proud and insulting, and you wanted to go away from her. Don't you remember?'

I said confusedly that that was long ago, and that I knew no better then, and the like. Estella smiled with perfect composure, and said she had no doubt of my having been quite right, and of her having been very disagreeable.

'Is *he* changed?' Miss Havisham asked her.

'Very much,' said Estella, looking at me.

'Less coarse and common?' said Miss Havisham, playing with Estella's hair.

Estella laughed, and looked at the shoe in her hand, and laughed again and looked at me, and put the shoe down. She treated me as a boy still, but she lured me on.

We sat in the dreamy room among the old strange influences which had so wrought upon me, and I learnt that she had but just come home from France, and that she was going to London. Proud and wilful as of old, she had brought those qualities into such subjection of her beauty that it was impossible and out of nature—or I thought so—to separate them from her beauty. Truly it was impossible to disassociate her presence from all those wretched hankerings after money and gentility that had disturbed my boyhood — from all those ill-regulated aspirations that had first made me ashamed of home and Joe—from all those visions that had raised her face in the glowing fire, struck it out of the iron on the anvil, extracted it from the darkness of night to look in at the wooden window of the forge and flit away. In a word, it was impossible for me to separate her, in the past or in the present, from the innermost life of my life.

It was settled that I should stay there all the rest of the day, and return to the hotel at night, and to London to-morrow. When we had conversed for a while, Miss Havisham sent us two out to walk in the neglected garden : on our coming in by-and-bye, she said I should wheel her about a little, as in times of yore.

So, Estella and I went out into the garden by the gate through which I had strayed to my encounter with the pale young gentleman, now Herbert; I, trembling in spirit and worshipping the very hem of her dress; she, quite composed and most decidedly not worshipping the hem of mine. As we drew near to the place of encounter, she stopped, and said :

'I must have been a singular little creature to hide and see that fight that day : but I did, and I enjoyed it very much.'

'You rewarded me very much.'

'Did I ?' she replied, in an incidental and forgetful way. 'I remember I entertained a great objection to your adversary, because I took it ill that he should be brought here to pester me with his company.'

'He and I are great friends now.'

'Are you ? I think I recollect, though, that you read with his father ?'

'Yes.'

I made the admittance with reluctance, for it seemed to have a boyish look, and she already treated me more than enough like a boy.

'Since your change of fortune and prospects, you have changed your companions,' said Estella.

'Naturally,' said I.

'And necessarily,' she added, in a haughty tone; 'what was fit company for you once, would be quite unfit company for you now.'

In my conscience, I doubt very much whether I had any lingering intention left of going to see Joe; but if I had, this observation put it to flight.

'You had no idea of your impending good fortune, in those times?' said Estella, with a slight wave of her hand, signifying the fighting times.

'Not in the least.'

The air of completeness and superiority with which she walked at my side, and the air of youthfulness and submission with which I walked at hers, made a contrast that I strongly felt. It would have rankled in me more than it did, if I had not regarded myself as eliciting it by being so set apart for her and assigned to her.

The garden was too overgrown and rank for walking in with ease, and after we had made the round of it twice or thrice, we came out again into the brewery yard. I showed her to a nicety where I had seen her walking on the casks, that first old day, and she said with a cold and careless look in that direction, 'Did I?' I reminded her where she had come out of the house and given me my meat and drink, and she said, 'I don't remember.' 'Not remember that you made me cry?' said I. 'No,' said she, and shook her head and looked about her. I verily believe her not remembering and not minding in the least, made me cry again, inwardly—and that is the sharpest crying of all.

'You must know,' said Estella, condescending to me as a brilliant and beautiful woman might, 'that I have no heart—if that has anything to do with my memory.'

I got through some jargon to the effect that I took the liberty of doubting that. That I knew better. That there could be no such beauty without it.

'Oh! I have a heart to be stabbed in or shot in, I have no doubt,' said Estella, 'and, of course, if it ceased to beat I should cease to be. But you know what I mean. I have no softness there, no—sympathy, —sentiment—nonsense.'

What *was* it that was borne in upon my mind when she stood still and looked attentively at me? Anything I had seen in Miss Havisham? No. In some of her looks and gestures there was that tinge of resemblance to Miss Havisham which may often be noticed to have been acquired by children, from grown persons with whom they have been much associated and secluded, and which, when childhood is past, will produce a remarkable, occasional likeness of expression between faces that are otherwise quite different. And yet I could not trace this to Miss Havisham. I looked again, and though she was still looking at me, the suggestion was gone.

What *was* it?

'I am serious,' said Estella, not so much with a frown (for her brow was smooth) as with a darkening of her face; 'if we are to be thrown much together, you had better believe it at once. No!' imperiously stopping me as I opened my lips. 'I have not bestowed my tenderness anywhere. I have never had any such thing.'

CHARLES DICKENS.

Great Expectations.

DR. PROUDIE may well be said to have been a fortunate man, for he was not born to wealth, and he is now Bishop of Barchester; but nevertheless he has his cares. He has a large family, of whom the three eldest are daughters, now all grown up and fit for fashionable life; and he has a wife. It is not my intention to breathe a word against the character of Mrs. Proudie, but still I cannot think that with all her virtues she adds much to her husband's happiness. The truth is that in matters domestic she rules supreme over her titular lord, and rules with a rod of iron. Nor is this all. Things domestic Dr. Proudie might have abandoned to her, if not voluntarily, yet willingly. But Mrs. Proudie is not satisfied with such home dominion, and stretches her power over all his movements, and will not even abstain from things spiritual. In fact, the bishop is henpecked.

The archdeacon's wife, in her happy home at Plumstead, knows how to assume the full privileges of her rank, and express her own mind in becoming tone and place. But Mrs. Grantly's sway, if sway she has, is easy and beneficent. She never shames her husband; before the world she is a pattern of obedience; her voice is never loud, nor her looks sharp; doubtless she values power, and has not unsuccessfully striven to acquire it; but she knows what should be the limits of a woman's rule.

Not so Mrs. Proudie. This lady is habitually authoritative to all, but to her poor husband she is despotic. Successful as has been his career in the eyes of the world, it would seem that in the eyes of his wife he is never right. All hope of defending himself has long passed from him; indeed he rarely even attempts self-justification; and is aware that submission produces the nearest approach to peace which his house can ever attain.

Mrs. Proudie has not been able to sit at the boards and committees to which her husband has been called by the state; nor, as he often reflects, can she make her voice heard in the House of Lords. It may be that she will refuse to him permission to attend to this branch of a bishop's duties; it may be that she will insist on his close attendance to his own closet. He has never whispered a word on the subject to living ears, but he has already made his fixed resolve. Should such an attempt be made he will rebel. Dogs have turned against their masters, and even Neapolitans against their rulers, when oppression has been too severe. And Dr. Proudie feels within himself that if the cord be drawn too tight, he also can muster courage and resist.

The state of vassalage in which our bishop has been kept by his wife has not tended to exalt his character in the eyes of his daughters, who assume in addressing their father too much of that authority

which is not properly belonging, at any rate, to them.
They are, on the whole, fine engaging young ladies.
They are tall and robust like their mother, whose
high cheek bones and—, we may say, auburn hair,
they all inherit. They think somewhat too much of
their grand uncles, who have not hitherto returned
the compliment by thinking much of them. But now
that their father is a bishop it is probable that family
ties will be drawn closer. Considering their connec-
tion with the church, they entertain but few prejudices
against the pleasures of the world; and have certainly
not distressed their parents, as too many English girls
have lately done, by any enthusiastic wish to devote
themselves to the seclusion of a protestant nunnery.
Dr. Proudie's sons are still at school.

One other marked peculiarity in the character of
the bishop's wife must be mentioned. Though not
adverse to the society and manners of the world, she
is in her own way a religious woman; and the form
in which this tendency shows itself in her is by a
strict observance of the Sabbatarian rule. Dissipa-
tion and low dresses during the week are, under her
control, atoned for by three services, an evening
sermon read by herself, and a perfect abstinence from
any cheering employment on the Sunday. Unfortun-
ately for those under her to whom the dissipation and
low dresses are not extended, her servants namely
and her husband, the compensating strictness of the
Sabbath includes all. Woe betide the recreant house-
maid who is found to have been listening to the

R

honey of a sweetheart in Regent's Park, instead of the soul-stirring evening discourse of Mr. Slope. Not only is she sent adrift, but she is also sent with a character which leaves her little hope of a decent place. Woe betide the six-foot hero who escorts Mrs. Proudie to her pew in red plush breeches, if he slips away to the neighbouring beer-shop, instead of falling into the back seat appropriated to his use. Mrs. Proudie has the eyes of Argus for such offenders. Occasional drunkenness in the week may be overlooked, for six feet on low wages are hardly to be procured if the morals are always kept at high pitch; but not even for grandeur or economy will Mrs. Proudie forgive a desecration of the Sabbath.

ANTHONY TROLLOPE.

Barchester Towers.

IT was far on in June now, and Maggie was inclined
to lengthen the daily walk which was her one indul-
gence ; but this day and the following she was so busy
with work which must be finished that she never went
beyond the gate, and satisfied her need of the open
air by sitting out of doors. One of her frequent walks,
when she was not obliged to go to St. Ogg's, was to a
spot that lay beyond what was called the 'Hill'—an
insignificant rise of ground crowned by trees, lying
along the side of the road which ran by the gates of
Dorlcote Mill. Insignificant I call it, because in
height it was hardly more than a bank ; but there may
come moments when Nature makes a mere bank a
means towards a fateful result, and this is why I ask
you to imagine this high bank crowned with trees,
making an uneven wall for some quarter of a mile
along the left side of Dorlcote Mill and the pleasant
fields behind it, bounded by the murmuring Ripple.
Just where this line of bank sloped down again to
the level, a by-road turned off and led to the other
side of the rise, where it was broken into very
capricious hollows and mounds by the working of an
exhausted stone-quarry—so long exhausted that both
mounds and hollows were clothed with brambles and
trees, and here and there by a stretch of grass which

a few sheep kept close-nibbled. In her childish days Maggie held this place, called the Red Deeps, in very great awe, and needed all her confidence in Tom's bravery to reconcile her to an excursion thither— visions of robbers and fierce animals haunting every hollow. But now it had the charm for her which any broken ground, any mimic rock and ravine, have for the eyes that rest habitually on the level; especially in summer, when she could sit on a grassy hollow under the shadow of a branching ash, stooping aslant from the steep above her, and listen to the hum of insects, like tiniest bells on the garment of Silence, or see the sunlight piercing the distant boughs, as if to chase and drive home the truant heavenly blue of the wild hyacinths. In this June time too, the dog-roses were in their glory, and that was· an additional reason why Maggie should direct her walk to the Red Deeps, rather than to any other spot, on the first day she was free to wander at her will—a pleasure she loved so well, in her ardours of renunciation, she thought she ought to deny herself the frequent indul-gence in it.

You may see her now, as she walks down the favourite turning, and enters the Deeps by a narrow path through a group of Scotch firs—her tall figure and old lavender-gown visible through an hereditary black silk shawl of some wide-meshed, net-like material; and now she is sure of being unseen, she takes off her bonnet and ties it over her arm. One would certainly suppose her to be farther on in life than her seventeenth year—perhaps because of the slow resigned sadness of the glance, from which all search and unrest seem to have departed, perhaps because her broad-chested figure has the mould of early womanhood. Youth and health have withstood the involuntary and voluntary hardships of her lot, and the nights in which she has lain on the hard floor for a penance have left no obvious trace; the eyes are liquid; the brown cheek is firm and rounded; the full lips are red. With her dark colouring and jet crown surmounting her tall figure, she seems to have a sort of kinship with the grand Scotch firs, at which she is looking up as if she loved them well. Yet one has a sense of uneasiness in looking at her—a sense of opposing elements, of which a fierce collision is imminent: surely there is a hushed expression, such as one often sees in older faces under the borderless caps, out of keeping with the resistant youth, which one expects to flash out in a sudden, passionate glance, that will dissipate all the quietude, like a damped fire leaping out again when all seemed safe.

But Maggie herself was not uneasy at this moment. She was calmly enjoying the free air, while she looked up at the old fir-trees, and thought that those broken ends of branches were the records of past storms, which had only made the red stems soar higher. But while her eyes were still turned upward, she became conscious of a moving shadow cast by the evening sun on the grassy path before her, and looked down with a startled gesture to see Philip Wakem, who first raised his hat, and then, blushing deeply, came forward to her and put out his hand. Maggie, too, coloured with surprise, which soon gave way to pleasure. She put out her hand and looked down at the deformed figure before her with frank eyes, filled for the moment with nothing but the memory of her child's feelings—a memory that was always strong in her. She was the first to speak.

'You startled me,' she said, smiling faintly; 'I never meet any one here. How came you to be walking here? Did you come to meet *me*?'

It was impossible not to perceive that Maggie felt herself a child again.

'Yes, I did,' said Philip, still embarrassed: 'I wished to see you very much. I watched a long while yesterday on the bank near your house to see if you would come out, but you never came. Then I watched again to-day, and when I saw the way you took, I kept you in sight and came down the bank, behind there. I hope you will not be displeased with me.'

'No,' said Maggie, with simple seriousness, walking on, as if she meant Philip to accompany her, 'I'm very glad you came, for I wished very much to have an opportunity of speaking to you. I've never forgotten how good you were long ago to Tom, and me too; but I was not sure that you would remember us so well. Tom and I have had a great deal of trouble since then, and I think *that* makes one think more of what happened before the trouble came.'

'I can't believe that you have thought of me so

much as I have thought of you,' said Philip, timidly. 'Do you know, when I was away, I made a picture of you as you looked that morning in the study when you said you would not forget me.'

Philip drew a large miniature case from his pocket, and opened it. Maggie saw her old self leaning on a table, with black locks hanging down behind her ears, looking into space with strange, dreamy eyes. It was a water-colour sketch, of real merit as a portrait.

'Oh dear,' said Maggie, smiling, and flushed with pleasure, 'what a queer little girl I was! I remember myself with my hair in that way, in that pink frock. I really *was* like a gypsy. I daresay I am now,' she added, after a little pause ; 'and am I like what you expected me to be ? '

The words might have been those of a coquette, but the full bright glance Maggie turned on Philip was not that of a coquette. She really did hope he liked her face as it was now, but it was simply the rising again of her innate delight in admiration and love. Philip met her eyes and looked at her in silence for a long moment, before he said, quietly, ' No, Maggie.'

The light died out a little from Maggie's face, and there was a slight trembling of the lip. Her eyelids fell lower, but she did not turn away her head, and Philip continued to look at her. Then he said, slowly—

' You are very much more beautiful than I thought you would be.'

'Am I?' said Maggie, the pleasure returning in a deeper flush. She turned her face away from him and took some steps, looking straight before her in silence, as if she were adjusting her consciousness to this new idea. Girls are so accustomed to think of dress as the main grounds of vanity, that, in abstaining from the looking-glass, Maggie had thought more of abandoning all care for adornment than of renouncing the contemplation of her face. Comparing herself with elegant, wealthy young ladies, it had not occurred to her that she could produce any effect with her person. Philip seemed to like the silence well. He walked by her side, watching her face, as if that sight left no room for any other wish.

GEORGE ELIOT.

The Mill on the Floss.

Text printed in Great Britain by T. and A. CONSTABLE, Printers to His Majesty, Edinburgh.

Illustrations printed by HENRY STONE AND SON, LTD., Banbury.

Lightning Source UK Ltd.
Milton Keynes UK
UKHW02f1158170518

322763UK00006B/861/P